From the *Mothers of Many Styles*™

# THE M.O.M.S.® HANDBOOK

**Second Edition**

*Understanding Your*

*Personality Type*

*In Mothering*

JANET P. PENLEY AND DIANE W. STEPHENS

Read thru pg 24 for 3/9

## OUR MISSION

*To inspire and empower mothers*
*to be their truest and best selves,*
*thereby promoting healing and balance*
*in our society and our children*

Mothers of Many Styles™
Penley and Associates, Inc.
604 Maple Ave.
Wilmette, IL 60091
847-251-4936 fax: 847-251-6998 website: http://www.momsconnection.com

ISBN 0-9646974-0-8

M.O.M.S.® and Mothers of Many Styles™ are trademarks of Penley and Associates, Inc.

Myers-Briggs Type Indicator and MBTI are registered trademarks of Consulting Psychologists Press, Inc.,
Palo Alto, California

Book design by Bookmark, Atlanta, Georgia
Second edition design and production by Creative Impulse Inc., Evanston, Illinois
Editing by Tom Thompson, Charleston, South Carolina
Illustration by Donna Reynolds, Oakland, California
Printed in the U.S.A.

# PART ONE

INFJ  Jennifer 5, 2
ISFJ  Janiece  9 mo. Emma
ISFJ  Racquel  8, 6, 4
              B  G  B

INFP  Cindy  8, 6
              G  G

# INTRODUCTION

*Dear Reader*

*M.O.M.S. was created by moms. Between the two of us, we are raising three daughters, one son, and two stepchildren.*

*We have been involved in ballet lessons, Little League, summer camp, PTA, Sunday School, soccer, car pools, laundry, fishsticks, homemade mashed potatoes, divorce and (lack of) child support, remarriage, the hiring and firing of child care providers, puberty, a second telephone line, boyfriends, college selection, combining paid work with family work...pretty much the gamut of the "total" mothering experience today.*

*M.O.M.S. was born of our personal struggles ... trying to be all things to all people. We listened to too many experts before beginning to trust who we really are and what's important to us. Over time and innumerable cups of coffee, we have come to let our inner wisdom and best, truest selves guide us toward being the most effective, loving mothers we can be for our children.*

*M.O.M.S. represents our own healing journey of increased self-esteem and respect for differences in others: our children, our husbands, our friends, our own mothers, and each other.*

*As mothers, we tend to focus on the development of our children, perhaps forgetting to attend to our own development. We have found it difficult, if not impossible, to instill good self-esteem in our children when our own sense of self is weak.*

*While we developed* The M.O.M.S. Handbook *from our own experience, it has benefited from the contributions of others through personal stories and examples, participation in research and programs, and encouragement. Our families have been wonderfully supportive.*

*In the three years since publication of the first edition of* The Handbook, *our work with mothers has expanded to include more experiences of parents around the world. This second edition of* The Handbook *features 16 pages of new information requested by readers on dads, co-parenting, and how to use type with children.*

*Our initial experience in different cultural, socio-economic, and age groups indicates that the core information on personality type and mothering is more valid than we would have guessed. As we look to future editions, we hope you will pass along comments that will help us address cross-cultural issues and broaden the applications even further.*

*M.O.M.S. and knowledge of psychological type have profoundly changed our lives by increasing our capacity to live and love. Our intent with this handbook is to pass along the gift. May something you learn have a positive effect on your life and relationships.*

*Sincerely,*

*Janet P. Penley*

*Janet P. Penley*

*Diane W. Stephens*

*Diane W. Stephens*

# *The Seven M.O.M.S. Principles*

## M.O.M.S. Is Based On These Principles:

**1** **Good mothers come in many styles.** There is no one right way to be a good mother, just as there is no one right way to be a good human being. As mothers, we each bring different strengths and interests to the job of mothering. The strengths of a woman's mothering style are partly determined by her unique personality, and she will have the most success and satisfaction when she turns her attention to her strengths rather than her shortcomings.

The good news is this: you no longer have to covet your neighbor's mothering style. You have your own style of mothering and your own strengths.

**2** **No mother is a perfect mother.** Believe it or not, no mother does all of the right things and none of the wrong things. No mother has the inside track on how to raise perfect children. Every mother, no matter how good she is, is a mixed bag. She has an undeniable human side comprised of limitations, needs, and vulnerabilities.

Fortunately, this is as it should be. Children don't need perfect mothers because, as human beings, they themselves will never be perfect either. Children need human mothers who can model for them how to make the most of their strengths, come to grips with their limitations, and manage their humanness to become the best they can be.

The reality is that the very qualities a woman perceives as her personal shortcomings are the flip side of the wonderful strengths that make her children lucky to have her as their mother.

**3** **There are no short cuts or quick fixes.** Experts, seminars, books, and well-meaning friends and family can provide new information, insights, perspectives, and skills for "better" mothering. But they never can be a replacement for a mother's own wisdom. To be a good mother and do her best by her children, a woman must find her own way rather than follow or copy somebody else's way. In the end, the good mother is the one who believes in herself and is willing to accept responsibility for her choices and decisions.

**4** **Nurturing your own self esteem is good for your child — as well as for you.** Anything a mother can do to nurture herself, heal old wounds, and increase her sense of being alright with the world has a positive impact on her children. Just as the mother who is breast feeding is aware of the connection between what she eats and drinks and what she is able to give her child, each mother must remember to "feed" herself emotionally and spiritually as well.

It's not self-indulgent for a woman to take good care of herself. It's healthy for her and lets her take better care of her children. Accepting and appreciating herself will help her accept and appreciate her children. When a woman allows herself to continue on her own journey of individuation, wholeness, and integrity, she opens the doors to greater potential for her children as well.

**5** **Differences are good.** Too often, when people are different, actions and messages become confused. A mother may think a child's or husband's behavior that's different from her own must be a way of trying to irritate her. ("I know he left his shoes in the middle of the living room floor again to let me know who's *really* in charge!") Usually though, it's just a case of seeing things differently and viewing life a different way. When a mother can accept differences — and begin to appreciate them — she may open herself to new messages and ways of loving.

**6** **Mothers are different from fathers.** A lot of M.O.M.S. information, but not all, can be applied to dads. "What About Dads?" on pages 44 to 47 explains how.

M.O.M.S. focuses on the mother as a unique person with a distinct personality, mixing the responsibilities of parenting with issues of what it means to be a woman "today." Each person has her own set of expectations for the role of mother and the role of father, many of which have been shaped or influenced by the broader society. Both gender and societal expectations keep us from being generic parenting machines.

Nevertheless, by focusing on the mother it is not M.O.M.S.' intent to exclude fathers or imply their role in the family is "less." In fact, we have wonderful memories and appreciate the role our fathers played in our lives. As we watch our children grow, we value and respect the unique contributions their fathers have made and continue to make.

**7 Mothering is important.** Even in these times of unprecedented opportunities and professional successes for women, probably no desire goes deeper, nor is a more powerful motivating force, than the desire to be a good mother. Being a good mother touches women's deepest needs for intimacy, competency, and generativity.

But society gives mixed messages about the importance of being a good mother. On the one hand, people will go to great lengths, physically and financially, to bear or adopt children. On the other, every woman knows that admitting she is at home all day raising children will not make her the center of attention at a social gathering.

Despite these cultural inconsistencies, we as mothers must learn to value the time and energy we devote to raising children — for each child's sake and for the sake of the next generation.

## M.O.M.S. and Personality Type

Mothers of Many Styles began in 1988 as a series of seminars and programs, primarily in the Chicago area. *The M.O.M.S. Handbook* is an attempt to make the core information developed for M.O.M.S. seminars more widely available...to women who are already aware of psychological type and to other professionals who work with parents and families.

M.O.M.S. is based on the personality framework developed by Carl Jung in his book *Psychological Types*. An American daughter-mother team — Isabel Briggs Myers and Katherine Briggs — built on Jung's theory and developed an inventory to help people identify their individual psychological types. Although there are other personality profiles, the Myers-Briggs Type Indicator (MBTI) has become the most widely used. It is popular in business (team development and management), career counseling, marriage enrichment, and education. It is one of the few psychological instruments developed for use with healthy, normal people.

Based on your personality preferences, M.O.M.S. can provide you with a more objective and realistic picture of your strengths, struggles, and needs as a mother, compared to all other mothers.

The connection between personality type and mothering style has been developed from more than 10 years of observation and study. This work includes experience with mothers from all over the country in more than 450 workshops, quantitative research with a sample of 600 mothers, and in-depth personal interviews with over 100 mothers.

However, neither M.O.M.S. nor psychological type can explain everything about you. Not all descriptions or examples will fit you or the way you live. When it comes to people, there are few simple answers. Especially for women. But if you are like most people, personality type will explain a lot about your unique gifts and differences.

# PART TWO

# THE BASICS OF PERSONALITY TYPE

M.O.M.S.' premise is this: appreciating your mothering style and making the most of it begins with self-knowledge.

This section is our starting point for self-knowledge. It features a brief overview of psychological type preferences, including definitions and descriptions. The information is summarized for easy review.

## The Basics of Personality Type

Where do you focus your attention, get your energy?

EXTRAVERSION    INTROVERSION

What information do you attend to most?

SENSING    INTUITION

How do you make judgments/decisions?

THINKING    FEELING

How do you like your outer world structured?

JUDGING    PERCEIVING

> *Which type is the most patient mother? In our interviews, we found no type mother thinks she has enough patience with her children. Different types were patient about different things. One might lose it over a cup of milk spilling and another over having to give long explanations.*

■ Personality type is identified by four letters. For example, ESTJ or INFP.

■ There are 16 combinations — 16 types.

■ Each type has its own uniqueness. There is a dynamic interaction between the four preferences that changes when even one preference is different.

■ American culture over-values some preferences — Extraversion, Sensing, and Judging — and undervalues Introversion, Intuition, and Perceiving. Our culture most prizes Thinking but expects women to be Feeling.

■ The frequency of each personality type in the population varies from 1% to 20%.

| PREFERENCE | DESCRIPTION | KEY WORDS | APPROXIMATE FREQUENCY IN U.S. POPULATION |
|---|---|---|---|
| EXTRAVERSION *(Energy)* | Energized by other people and things, external experiences<br>Expressive, easy to know<br>Prefers activity; wants to contribute to the action<br>Likes to process externally: talk things out | Outward<br>Many<br>People<br>Action<br>Breadth | 60% |
| INTROVERSION | Energized by the inner world of ideas and reflection<br>Contained, reserved<br>Prefers solitude and calm; likes working alone<br>Likes to process internally: think things through | Inward<br>Few<br>Privacy<br>Reflections<br>Depth | 40% |
| SENSING *(Information)* | The five senses<br>Lives in the here and now, enjoying what's there<br>Concrete, what is real<br>Takes a step-by-step approach | Realistic<br>Details<br>Present<br>Common Sense<br>Facts | 75% |
| INTUITION | The sixth sense, hunches<br>Lives toward the future, anticipating what might be<br>Abstract, what could be<br>Usually proceeds by leaping around; bursts of energy | Imaginative<br>Patterns<br>Future<br>Theory<br>Innovation | 25% |
| THINKING *(how we make decisions)* | Decides with the head<br>Concerned for truth, justice, fairness<br>Skeptical, takes nothing for granted<br>Values and trusts logic | Head<br>Firm and fair<br>Analyze<br>Justice<br>Objective<br>Critique | Women: 40%<br>Men: 60% *gender bias* |
| FEELING | Decides with the heart<br>Concerned with relationships, harmony<br>Praiseful and accepting<br>Values and trusts gut feelings | Heart<br>Compassionate<br>Empathize<br>Harmony<br>Subjective<br>Compliment | Women: 60%<br>Men: 40% |
| JUDGING *(lifestyle (how we structure of lifestyle))* | Plans provide comfort and security<br>Aims to structure one's life<br>Likes to do one thing at a time<br>Wants to be prepared, not caught by surprise | Structure<br>Closure<br>Planful<br>Organized<br>Control | 60% |
| PERCEIVING | Plans cut off unexpected opportunities<br>Aims to let life happen<br>Most productive doing several things at once<br>Likes to take things as they come; responds<br>    well to the unexpected | Flow<br>Openness<br>Spontaneous<br>Flexible<br>Adapt | 40% |

# PART THREE

# YOUR TYPE PREFERENCES
# AND MOTHERING STYLE

Perhaps you like being on the go ... and you think nothing of taking your children along to enjoy it with you. Maybe you find it difficult to listen to your son as he thinks out loud — you're annoyed by the unnecessary talking. Perhaps nothing brings you more pleasure than just "hanging out" with your children. Or it could be that you're fidgety and anxious if you leave all that needs to be done to play with your pre-schooler at the park.

There's a reason one woman's treat is another's torture — your personality preferences in each of the four categories:

• Extraversion-Introversion: energy
• Sensing-Intuition: information
• Thinking-Feeling: decision-making
• Judging-Perceiving: lifestyle

Some aspects of being a mother are likely to come naturally to you and be a pleasure. Others are going to be a struggle, and you'll find them draining.

This section looks at each preference individually, proceeding step by step in outlining strengths, struggles, and simple strategies for making the most of your personality preference. Specific tips for self-care are included, so you'll have energy to do your best mothering and ideas for responding to loved ones who have different personality preferences than yours.

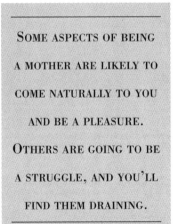

SOME ASPECTS OF BEING A MOTHER ARE LIKELY TO COME NATURALLY TO YOU AND BE A PLEASURE. OTHERS ARE GOING TO BE A STRUGGLE, AND YOU'LL FIND THEM DRAINING.

In this section, you are being asked to sort yourself into one of two groups for each function. Do you have a preference for Thinking or Feeling, for example? The purpose is to give you an in-depth understanding of the individual preferences. However, as you read over the strengths and struggles for each of your preferences, you may find that some do not seem to apply to who you are.

Here are two possible reasons you can consider:

First, we are all more than any one of our individual preferences. As your four preferences combine, the interaction among two or more preferences may determine how well you relate to a particular description. For example, if you have a preference for both Introversion and Thinking, you may identify more readily with Introverted characteristics than if you have a preference for Introversion and Feeling. The unique dynamics of your individual personality type are addressed in Part Four.

Second, the strength of your preference on each dimension is bound to vary. Two women may both be ENFPs, but one may have a strong preference for Extraversion while the other has only a slight preference for Extraversion. It is likely that the first ENFP will relate to more items on the Extraverted type descriptions than the second. There are many individual differences between people of the same personality type.

# *Extraversion and Introversion*

Most mothers say they do their best mothering when they're full of energy. And they're most likely to do or say something they'll regret when they're feeling tired and drained.

How can you maintain a comfortable level of energy?

An understanding of what gives you energy and what drains your energy — your preference for Extraversion or Introversion — is a good place to start.

Extraverted mothers are energized by people, action, and variety. Introverted mothers are energized by focusing inward, which requires private space, absence of people, and silence.

Because motherhood is synonymous with people, Extraverted mothers are more likely to have the energy to keep up with their children most of the day.

Introverted mothers tend to tire out during the day without some alone time. Unfortunately, they too often regard "time alone" as a luxury, not a necessity, and they spend much of the day feeling tense, tired, and ready to snap.

Somewhat surprisingly, many Extraverted mothers say they relate to descriptions of the Introverted mother. Having small children constantly underfoot, balancing career and family, or trying to keep up with active teens is so demanding, even Extraverted mothers may feel over-extraverted and close to burnout. They too need quiet time toward the end of the day before going out with friends or joining in family fun.

And they like it! Motherhood and family life have stretched them to develop their introspection, getting to know themselves better and discovering more of their inner wisdom.

Similarly, some Introverts say becoming a mother has helped them develop their outward focus. Growing up, Introverts may have been more comfortable as loners. Then along came motherhood, complete with babysitting co-ops, play groups, PTA, and carpools . . . not to mention their children's people needs.

Now they enjoy an active family life . . . but in smaller doses than Extraverted mothers, remembering to claim the time alone they need everyday to manage their energy.

## *The Extraverted Mother*

MAY GRAVITATE TOWARD . . .

■ Getting out and taking young children along to experience the world

■ Being on the go, involved in a variety of activities; thriving at a busy pace

■ Providing her children with opportunities to be with people

■ Enjoying casual conversations with children; feeling free to ask them questions

■ Connecting with and tuning in to the world beyond the home; being "in the know" when it comes to community, school, volunteer organizations, and the neighborhood

■ Providing the spark to get things going and keep things moving; serving as an example of get-up-and-go

■ Teaching her children the importance of social skills and graces . . . so they can get along in the world

■ Connecting with the people and high energy of large family gatherings

## The **Extraverted** Mother May Struggle With . . .

■ Being isolated at home with babies and preschoolers

■ Tuning out societal and other external expectations

■ Worrying whether her children have enough friends and/or activities

■ Overextending: not limiting her children's and her own involvement to meaningful activities

■ Respecting a child's personal space; not being intrusive

■ Listening rather than talking; not dominating a conversation with a child

■ Understanding, accepting, or encouraging a child's need for alone time . . . particularly an Introverted child

## Tips For The **Extraverted** Mother

*"Taking care of me" means having variety, action, and people to recharge.*

■ Don't allow yourself to become isolated at home. This is particularly important for first-time mothers. Some kind of employment or joining a group can be what you need to feel connected with others. Consider a Saturday evening on the town or a day with friends.

■ But don't overdo. Learn when you've had enough and how to say "no." Limit your activities to those that are the most meaningful.

■ Consider taking an enforced "stay-at-home" day once a week . . . to balance being on the go.

■ Don't expect your partner or children to meet all your needs for Extraversion, particularly if any of them are Introverts. Enjoy a night out with your friends, leaving dad at home with the kids. Likewise, leave your young Introverted child at home with a babysitter or older sibling while you run errands.

■ Have faith that your Introverted child will turn out alright. You can encourage playmates and activities, but Introverts do best with people when their need for solitude is met first.

■ Spend time alone getting to know yourself and discovering your needs and opinions separate from your family's and society's.

■ Slow down. Your self-worth is in who you are, not what you do.

*Illustration from Parenting Style Slide Set*

*When asked to name their strengths, many Extraverted mothers mention "energy." They have energy to juggle people and activities. Children, work, and leisure also energize the Extravert. They make her feel alive and connected to the world.*

## *The Introverted Mother*

### May Gravitate Toward . . .

■ Being observant and reflective about her children in an effort to know each child in-depth

■ Encouraging her children not to overextend by providing the time and space for a child's "down time"

■ Respecting and understanding a child's need for time alone

■ Respecting a child who's not one of the crowd

■ Providing a quiet and calming presence (although inside she may not feel calm)

■ Tuning out distractions, concentrating on one child or one thing at a time

■ Limiting extraneous involvements to focus more exclusively on her family

■ Standing back and watching her children be active and interact on their own — without dominating or intruding; staying in the background

### The **Introverted** Mother May Struggle With . . .

■ Being simultaneously focused on children, the tasks at hand, and other external matters . . . beyond her natural limits

■ Handling a large family or large groups of children

■ Finding the energy to maintain the pace of active young children and adolescents

> *An Extraverted mother from a highly Extraverted family has an Introverted daughter. At family get-togethers, the young girl would ask her Extraverted grandmother to leave the group and join her one-on-one in a separate room to read a book. Over time this troubled the grandmother, and she finally questioned the mother about what could be "wrong" with the child. Knowing type, the mother explained that her daughter was drained, not energized, by the large groups of people. The grandmother now understands and not only respects her granddaughter's need for time alone, she no longer insists that her granddaughter stay with the party.*

■ Responding "on the spot" to children's unexpected requests; not having the time she needs to think things through

■ Being as emotionally or cognitively accessible to her children as she thinks she should be (she may seem detached and "aloof")

■ Understanding an Extraverted child's need to be on the go with friends and activities

■ Accepting an Extravert's need to think out loud (she may be irritated by "unnecessary talking")

## TIPS FOR THE **INTROVERTED** MOTHER

*"Taking care of me" means getting quiet time for reflection and recharging energy.*

■ Take at least a half hour to an hour every day for solitude. Ignore the popular notion that time sitting quietly is non-productive, a luxury when everything else is done.

■ Be creative in your quest for solitude. Hire a babysitter to take small children to the park while you enjoy the quiet at home. When babies are napping, avoid phone calls, household chores, or any other intrusions or distractions. Get up early before your work day begins, or stay up late after children and teens are in bed.

■ Find ways that don't involve you to meet your young child's need for external stimulation. Consider play groups, extra classes, and programs where other adults are in charge. Bring in a mother's helper or grandma to play with your child. Or ask an older sibling to help.

■ If you have a very Extraverted child, set boundaries to protect your needs for Introversion and his or her needs to interact with you. Retreat to solitude before you reach your limit. You'll avoid exploding and feeling guilty afterwards.

■ Learn a comfortable way to respond to children's unexpected requests. Share a bit of your unfinished thoughts while also giving yourself the time you need to think things through. Practice saying, for example, "My initial thoughts are . . . , but I need more time to think it over. I'll give you my decision at dinner."

■ Practice ways of saying "no" to events and commitments that require too much extraversion. Keep a list of responses by the phone: "Rather than chaperone the dance, could I drop off refreshments instead?" or "My schedule is busy. Could you put me down for next month?"

■ Claim the strengths of your Introverted preference — the ability to connect with the depth of life. Being in the minority, you may feel inadequate or energyless if you compare yourself to active, on-the-go Extraverted moms.

*Illustration from Parenting Style Slide Set*

*Noise, confusion, and never-ending demands for her attention can make an Introverted mother feel she's about to explode. Though she'd rather turn inward, mothering requires her to maintain an outward focus. The result can be overstimulation and exhaustion.*

# *Sensing and Intuition*

What kind of information do you trust most about your children? Facts or impressions?

The kind of "information" you attend to as a mother is largely determined by your preference for Sensing or Intuition.

Sensing mothers are most comfortable with information they acquire from the five senses — the facts. The Intuitive mother is more comfortable with what she gleans from her "sixth" sense — impressions.

These different approaches to information-gathering manifest themselves in a variety of ways when it comes to mothering styles. For example, Sensing mothers are likely to stick to what's tried-and-true, while Intuitive mothers like to experiment. Sensing mothers may be at home with notions of "experience," "practicalities," and "what is." Intuitive mothers resonate with "newness," "theory," and "what could be."

Characteristics of the Sensing preference can vary dramatically, depending on whether Sensing is coupled with the Judging or Perceiving preference. Both Sensing-Judging (SJ) and Sensing-Perceiving (SP)

mothers are down-to-earth, but they are very different.

The SJ mother is typically adept at providing security, doing "for" her children, and providing what a parent "should." She tends to be traditional in her approach to mothering and strives for daily routines designed to assure stability and consistency in her child's life.

The SP mother prefers to live in the moment, giving her children a spontaneous response to their needs, and probably having more fun. She bristles at routine and would rather enjoy life as it comes; she may identify with many of the Intuitive's struggles.

Characteristics of the Intuitive preference can also vary, depending on whether it is combined with the preference for Feeling or Thinking. Both Intuitive-Feeling (NF) and Intuitive-Thinking (NT) mothers focus on possibilities and the "big picture." NFs are adept at "tuning in" to a child at his or her level, often playfully. NTs are skilled at teaching and relate to their children on an intellectual, adult level.

## *The Sensing Mother*

### MAY GRAVITATE TOWARD . . .

■ Taking care of the basic needs of her children, seeing that they're well fed, clean, rested, and healthy, and that they have transportation

■ "Being there" physically for her children

■ Giving her children a hands-on, practical understanding of how to get along in the world

■ Showing care in concrete ways: favorite desserts for each family member at Thanksgiving, a filled gas tank for a special date, playing a child's board game

■ Providing children with rich sensory experiences: gym and play rooms, sight-seeing, afternoons in the park, ball games, gardening

■ Valuing and conveying the importance of family traditions

■ Putting importance on the practical side of intelligence: getting the facts straight, common sense, and applied knowledge

■ Keeping life simple and grounded in the here-and-now ("There's no such thing as ghosts." "Don't borrow trouble." "Don't worry, be happy.")

■ Creating comfortable physical surroundings and home environment for her family

## THE SENSING MOTHER MAY STRUGGLE WITH . . .

■ Appreciating or joining in with a child's imagination and fantasy

■ Being overly focused on details and small incidents

■ Understanding a child who's different from the "norm" or different from her

■ Seeing possibilities in complicated or difficult situations, such as a child not getting dressed in the morning or an adolescent bringing home bad grades; not feeling stuck

■ Feeling overwhelmed or stressed out by all the details and things to do, such as preparing for a family gathering, getting kids back to school, or cleaning up a huge mess

■ Appreciating an Intuitive child's "big picture" orientation; not making him or her feel impractical, unobservant, or "flaky"

## TIPS FOR THE SENSING MOTHER

*"Taking care of me" means feeding my senses — avoiding sensory deprivation.*

■ Use a friend as a "consultant" for seeing things in a new way. Or try a mother support group, books on child rearing, or professional help if you're stumped.

> **A** *Sensing mother with an Intuitive son was having difficulty getting her son out the door, into the car, and on their way to preschool. One snowy January day, he was dawdling as usual and ignoring her "it's time to go" warnings. Remembering Intuitives prefer enthusiastic and imaginative communication, she went outside and called to him: "Come, let's go for a ride in my snow chariot." He raced out the door and hopped in the car, with a smile on his face.*

■ Give the Intuitives in your life the time and space they need to play with ideas and dream without criticism or pressure to be practical. Wait until later to ask about the specifics and practicalities — they'll be more receptive once they've had a chance to fully explore the possibilities.

■ Don't feel compelled to join in your child's fantasy play if you don't feel like it. He or she will find friends, books, and games that can stimulate his or her imagination.

*Most mothers want to "be there" for their children. But the Sensing mother wants to "be there," literally. Only when she's physically present at the playground, school, and after-school activities can she do things for her children or with them.*

■ Try "brainstorming" as a playful way to consider new possibilities. For example, sit down with your child and try to come up with 20 ideas of "fun" activities to do together. Or make a list of 10 ways to solve a problem. The ideas can be impractical and even absurd. Be sure to withhold any evaluations until the list is complete. Then go back and consider each one, listening to each person's viewpoint. Usually one or two will make sense.

■ If you're a Sensing-Judging mother, routinize pleasurable, sensory-rich experiences that keep you

fresh. Set aside a definite time daily or several times a week for needlework, gardening, soaking in a bubblebath, working out, or taking a walk with a friend.

■ If you're a Sensing-Perceiving mother, consider an enforced "taking care of business" day once a week — it can vary from week to week — just to get errands done and keep the real world of schedules and routines from overwhelming you. Or consider getting regular help setting the house in order; it may be just the task your Sensing-Judging mate, son, or daughter was looking for.

## The Intuitive Mother

### MAY GRAVITATE TOWARD . . .

■ Valuing and encouraging creativity and imagination in all forms: making up games, pretending, crafts, book-making, inventions, composing music, attending cultural and artistic events

■ Pointing up options and possibilities, offering children choices, encouraging a new twist on the tried-and-true

■ Looking for and encouraging the unique potential in each child — valuing individuality and independent thinking

■ Bringing an imaginative and novel approach to the ordinary and routine

■ Explaining ideas, insights, perspectives, and meanings behind everyday experiences

■ Valuing her child's quickness of understanding, insight into complexity, and flashes of originality

■ Seeking out new techniques and perspectives on parenting

■ Keeping sight of the "big picture" — seeing different sides of an issue, many possibilities and complications, not just life in black-and-white

■ Valuing mothering as a personal growth experience, a catalyst for developing her own unique potential

### THE **INTUITIVE** MOTHER MAY STRUGGLE WITH . . .

■ Unrealistic expectations; feeling inadequate and discouraged with herself and her family when "real life" falls short of the "ideal"

*An Intuitive mother was having problems getting her Sensing-Perceiving daughter to put away her toys before bedtime. Remembering that SPs like fun and action, the mother devised a "Treasure Hunt Game." She hid pennies under piles of toys and clothes. A half hour before bedtime, her daughter could play the game — discover the buried treasure, which could only be found as the room became uncluttered.*

*The Intuitive mother takes great pleasure in her children's creativity. An innovator herself, she often encourages imagination by building on their ideas and joining in. If the game is dress-up, she may suggest they put on a play and give herself a role as well.*

■ Living in the here-and-now, taking pleasure in the moment

■ Keeping things simple. She may make it more complicated than it needs to be.

■ Knowing how much time and detailed effort a task will take, whether it's getting ready for a trip or mending a shirt (usually she underestimates, but sometimes she overestimates)

■ Giving a child detailed, specific instructions

■ Appreciating a Sensing child's step-by-step, practical approach to learning; not making him or her feel slow or mundane

## TIPS FOR THE **INTUITIVE** MOTHER

*"Taking care of me" means entertaining new ideas, perspectives, and dreams.*

■ Get a better idea of how much time the basics of day-to-day living really take: time yourself with a timer. Then you'll know how long it takes to drive to school or sew on a button, and you can use this real-life information to plan next time.

■ Use "play" as a way to develop your Sensing function and capacity for concrete information. Developing one's non-preferences is best done just for fun without pressure to succeed. Children can be great encouragers and "playmates" of such Sensing-type activities as jig-saw puzzles and drawing.

■ The next time you want to change "the way we do things around here," consider making moderate refinements rather than sweeping improvements. Instead of eliminating junk food from the family diet forever, you'll have more success if you down-scale to a one-sweet-per-day rule.

■ Have faith in your Sensing child's intelligence and brightness. He or she approaches learning differently than you do and has different interests. Take pleasure in her ability to set the clock on the VCR or his speed in reciting the multiplication tables in 187 seconds.

■ Enjoy living in the moment. Not everything you're doing *now* needs to be in preparation for tomorrow ... or the next day ... or when the kids are getting ready for college. Set aside several minutes each day just to take pleasure in what *is*.

■ Do a little rather than nothing. Many Intuitives say they shy away from doing something that seems small but is really part of a bigger project, whether it's putting one file folder away (because the whole filing system needs to be reorganized) or sweeping the kitchen floor (because the cabinets and walls need scrubbing). Don't let yourself become immobilized by the idea that "there isn't enough time to get into it now and do it right." If it's the first warm, sunny day of spring, taking five minutes to enjoy the sunshine is better than staying indoors because you don't have time to take a picnic to the park.

*I may be more of a thinker when it comes to mothering!*

# Thinking and Feeling

Motherhood is charged with numerous "shoulds" when it comes to the Thinking-Feeling function. No other function is so loaded. When defining a "good" mother, Thinking and Feeling mothers often misunderstand and devalue each other.

The bottom line is ... Thinking and Feeling mothers are equally "good." The difference is, they bring different strengths to mothering.

Thinking and Feeling represent preferences for two styles of making judgments and decisions. Of course, we all think and we all feel. The preference for Thinking or Feeling indicates whether you tend to lead with your head or your heart.

Our culture, however, overvalues Thinking and has traditionally associated Thinking with men and Feeling with women. Statistically, preference distributions by gender are not extreme: women 60% Feeling, 40% Thinking, and men 60% Thinking, 40% Feeling.

Today's mothers grew up when it was expected that girls would have a preference for Feeling — be relationship-oriented, personal, and warm.

Girls with a preference for Thinking — logic, analysis, and objectivity — often felt out of the mainstream. With gender-based cultural pressures, many learned how and when to function in traditionally feminine and Feeling ways. As a result, many Thinking women embody Feeling characteristics Thinking men are not necessarily encouraged to develop.

Women today are expected to be equally comfortable and competent in both the Thinking and Feeling modes. Many of us are confused.

Motherhood is an opportunity to sort out your natural way and use enhanced self-knowledge to your best advantage. This life-changing experience may also help you tune out societal pressures to be something you're not.

Just as important, motherhood may stretch you to cultivate some of the strengths of your opposite to meet the changing needs of your growing children. Typically, a Thinking mother may make a conscious effort to meet a young child's needs for closeness and affection. A Feeling mother may decide to take on a more objective viewpoint to meet a maturing child's need for independence.

Knowing your preference on the Thinking-Feeling dimension lets you realize where you stand in the context of cultural pressures. Knowing what comes naturally to you can inform your decisions and help you eliminate some of the guilt, stress, and conflict inherent in mothering on a day-to-day basis. It will let you honor your strengths (knowing they're but one piece of the truth) and help you relax, observe, appreciate, and learn a piece of the truth from your neighbor with the opposite preference.

## The Thinking Mother

### MAY GRAVITATE TOWARD . . .

■ Giving her children the physical and psychological space they need to stand on their own two feet and become independent

■ Helping her children analyze situations and problem-solve

■ Encouraging her children to do for themselves, promoting self-reliance and self-sufficiency

■ Paying attention to how her children think things through, encouraging them to think for themselves ... to think independently

■ Fostering ongoing intellectual development — curiosity, love of learning, mental challenges — by talking, teaching, discussing issues on a mature level, answering her children's whys

■ Encouraging competency and a can-do attitude, helping them excel in school, do their best, and work up to standards

■ Having confidence in a child's accomplishments, emphasizing achievements and their successes

■ Encouraging children to seek justice and fairness in all situations

■ Relying on logical consequences and cause-and-effect as a method of teaching and modifying behavior

■ Dealing with issues in a straightforward manner as they arise, maintaining perspective and rationality

■ Providing children with a role model for a competent, independent woman

■ Feeling best suited to the needs of older children, relishing frank and meaty discussions

## THE THINKING MOTHER MAY STRUGGLE WITH . . .

■ Tuning in to and being patient with feelings . . . especially those that seem irrational, are "going nowhere," or have no basis in reality. ("What do you mean you don't feel loved — you *are* loved.")

■ Accepting a child as he or she is, not being critical or expecting greater success

■ Feeling comfortable and confident with a clingy, needy child, fearing he or she will never be independent

■ Picking up on cues in delicate situations, not bulldozing or being "heavy handed"

■ Maintaining energy for lengthy, emotionally charged discussions pertaining to her personal issues or relationships within the family

■ Hanging in there with situations where there's no clear-cut answer or solution

■ Not sounding harsh

*Illustration from Parenting Style Slide Set*

*The Thinking mother can use even difficult situations to demonstrate objective analysis and logical problem- solving. Though tempted to jump in and dispense justice herself, she is more likely to provide principles so children can resolve matters on their own.*

## Tips For The **Thinking** Mother

*"Taking care of me" means getting
validation of my competence.*

■ Put your skills and talents to use on behalf of a
volunteer organization or in an employment setting.
You need objective measures of your competence —
concrete accomplishments, measurable achievements,
performance evaluations, raises, promotions — which
are hard to find (or non-existent) in the personal
realm of home and family.

■ Remember to validate the competence of your
children. Neither you nor they can take it for granted.
Since one of the Thinker's strengths is honest, truthful
feedback, you may be perceived as "critical." When
your 10-year-old asks you to review her book report,
be sure to balance criticisms and suggestions for
improvement with a healthy dose of appreciation and
praise for what she has accomplished on her own.

■ Have confidence that even the most "dependent"
children become independent. Don't worry about
your "clinging" three-year-old or kindergartner who
has trouble separating. Feel free to relax and enjoy
how much they want you. Children need to have
their needs for attachment met and feel secure in
your love before they can begin to disengage and
become truly independent.

■ When you're problem-solving, remember that
feelings have as much validity as do facts and logic.
Think of feelings as another criterion to be factored
into the equation.

■ Don't rush the healing process. Hurt feelings
need time to hurt for a while. So do painful issues
— like career changes or letting your 24-year-old

*Feeling mothers often express concern that
their Thinking children and/or Thinking
spouses seem "insensitive" and "uncaring."
And Thinking mothers are often uncomfortable initiating or participating in conversations about feelings. Some Feeling
and Thinking mothers have had success
"quantifying" feelings to ease their situations. One Thinking mother told her
Thinking son, "I'm only 25% mad that
you forgot to make your bed." A Feeling
mother asked her Thinking daughter,
"On a scale of one to 10, how upset are
you about not making the soccer team?"
A Thinking mother asked her Feeling
preschooler, "How many hugs would it
take to make you feel better?"*

move back home. Just like you can't instantly heal a
scraped knee, you can't fix everything. In fact, solving
a problem too quickly can cut off both the natural
healing process and the best solution.

■ Know that you are loved for who you are — not
for your competence. You don't have to prove yourself
to be loved by your children. That's your birthright
as a mother.

## The Feeling Mother

### MAY GRAVITATE TOWARD . . .

■ Giving her children the physical and emotional closeness they need to feel loved, special, and secure

■ Paying attention to how children feel; being sensitive, sympathetic, and comforting

■ Tuning in and being responsive to her children's needs — giving and doing for them

■ Fostering family harmony by encouraging and expecting cooperation, accommodation, and give-and-take

■ Going to great lengths to make her children happy, aiming to please (even if it means self-sacrifice)

■ Taking delight when her child expresses appreciation, affirmation, and acceptance of her

■ Seeing mothering as the "grandest intimacy," an opportunity to experience a special connectedness that is not possible in any other relationship

■ Encouraging her children to get along with others; promoting consideration, sympathy, and consensus

■ Looking for what's good in a child; accepting and affirming

> INSTEAD OF EXPECTING FAMILY HARMONY ALL THE TIME, SET THE GOAL AT 80% . . . FOR THE SAKE OF INTIMACY. SHOWING LOVE MEANS HONORING HOW YOU FEEL AND SOMETIMES SAYING WHAT YOU THINK EVEN IF IT RESULTS IN CONFLICT.

■ Sharing and confiding; initiating "heart to heart" talks — frequently

■ Protecting her children from life's "hard knocks" and the consequences of their actions

■ Feeling well-suited to the needs of younger children, possibly feeling like a "natural" mother early on

### THE FEELING MOTHER MAY STRUGGLE WITH . . .

■ Keeping her emotions separate from her children's issues — being devastated by a child's hurts or manipulated by her children's anger or lovingness

■ Getting her own needs identified and met (she may be prone to giving too much and then feeling unappreciated and taken for granted)

■ Confrontation — saying "no", being direct and firm, especially when it may cause disharmony and friction

■ Dealing with multiple wants and constant demands, when "everyone in the family is needing something at the same time"

■ Separating from her children too frequently or when she feels her children are too young

■ Holding her children too close, smothering, finding it hard to let go and back off

■ Feeling guilty whenever her attention has not been 100% on her children's needs

*Illustration from Parenting Style Slide Set*

*With her focus on relationships and harmony, the Feeling mother believes mother-child togetherness is the foundation which allows children to blossom. She likes to remind her children of their connection even when they're apart.*

## TIPS FOR THE **FEELING** MOTHER

*"Taking care of me" means taking a break from caring for other people's needs, putting my own needs first.*

■ Find out what your own needs really are. Mothers (especially Feeling mothers) often forget what they need, because they're so concerned with tending to others' needs. Perhaps you like pepperoni on your pizza, or maybe you long for a day to curl up with a stack of magazines. Remembering what used to nourish you before you had so many responsibilities is a good place to start.

■ Remind yourself that focusing on your needs can be *good* for your children. When not totally tuned in to their children, many Feeling mothers say they feel guilty and believe their children will suffer. Or they question whether they're being selfish. Actually, taking the focus off your children and putting it on you teaches your children respect for you. It gives a clear message of *your* self-worth.

■ If you can't see your way clear through an emotionally laden situation, use your frustration as a signal to get some help. Imagine yourself an outsider looking in. Or get a Thinking friend to consult with you.

■ Instead of expecting family harmony all the time, set the goal at 80% ... for the sake of intimacy. Sibling bickering may be a sign of a truly loving relationship. No two people (much less three or four or more) can be perfectly in sync all the time. Showing love means honoring how you feel and sometimes saying what you think even if it results in conflict.

■ Don't expect your Thinking child to be as comfortable with feelings as you are. You can't look for the same signals of caring as you would with a Feeling child. Rather than offer hugs and kisses or sharing feelings, your Thinking child may show her love through responsibility, respect, persistent questions, and honest feedback.

# *Judging and Perceiving*

Of all four functions, Judging-Perceiving is the one where every woman stretches considerably to develop her opposite as she delves into the day-to-day demands of motherhood. It seems the more people in your family, the more organized *and* more flexible you need to be.

Judging-Perceiving is about lifestyle — how you like your outer world structured. There's nothing like children to change your outer world and turn it upside down.

Judging women say that, before children, they could stick to a plan no matter what, keep their living space well ordered, and maintain "control" over most aspects of their lives. With children, many point out that their plans frequently go up in smoke and that they have very little control over what their children do.

Similarly, Perceiving mothers say that, before children, they lived life on the spur of the moment, they could pack for trips at the last minute, and they could be casual about some commitments.

With children, many point out that the school bus leaves *on time* and their children are held accountable to schedules and commitments in a Judging world.

Time is an issue for both Judging and Perceiving mothers, but they approach it differently. Responding to an internal clock as well as external pressures, Judging mothers are at home with notions of "promptness," "deadlines," and "schedules." They know how to make the most of time.

Perceiving mothers are less driven by an internal schedule and the need to quantify what can be done in a certain time frame. They view time less literally and are more comfortable just living in the process. They know how to make the most of the moment.

As a mother, developing your Judging-Perceiving opposite has a couple of important advantages. You can know when to make the most of time and when to make the most of the moment. And you can know when to take control and when to let go.

## *The Judging Mother*

MAY GRAVITATE TOWARD . . .

■ Organizing and planning day-to-day living so her children don't miss out — permission slips, lunch money, snack for snack day, kindergarten registration, school physicals

■ Keeping her children on an even keel with set mealtimes, bedtimes, and family routines

■ Being directive and setting limits. She's willing to call the shots when she thinks it's in the best interest of her child

■ Guiding and shaping her children and who they become

■ Approaching mothering as a serious responsibility; working hard, aiming to do the "right" thing, being conscientious and intense

■ Making a smooth-running, orderly household a high priority; factoring in housework as part of the weekly schedule

■ Showing children how to get a lot done — organization, planning, focus, discipline, and follow-through — by teaching and by doing

■ Encouraging children to respect and use their time wisely — time management, when is the right time for this and not this, deadlines, punctuality, respect for others' schedules

## The **Judging** Mother May Struggle With . . .

■ Living with the never-completed aspects of mothering; being comfortable with the ongoing process of raising children

■ Adapting to the unexpected and coping with last-minute changes that "blow the plan"

■ Letting go of "shoulds" and needing to have things done the "right" way

■ Relaxing and having fun when things still need to get done

■ Giving up control, so her children can take increasing control of their own lives

■ Hearing children out, not making snap judgments

■ Not accomplishing as much as she wants and expects to — "If it weren't for the kids ..."

■ Functioning in the midst of children's clutter, disorder, commotion, and messes

■ Backing off to let a Perceiving child have flexibility

## Tips For The **Judging** Mother

*"Taking care of me" means having a place
or project of my own to control, organize,
and complete.*

■ Claim one room or area of the house as your own — a place where you can keep things your way. Perhaps it's the top kitchen cupboards or a desk. Or, if you need to get out of the house to truly satisfy your desire for structure and organization, take on a project or job where you can create your own order.

> *A Judging mother sent her Perceiving son to the store to pick up some bread. She waited and waited, partly angry that he was taking too long and partly worried that something had happened to him. When he returned home, safely, she scolded him for being gone so long. He replied, "Next time, just estimate how long you think it should take. Multiply by two, and I'll always be on time."*

■ When you're frustrated at not being able to control what your children do, focus on organizing and coming to closure on projects that are under your control — emptying wastepaper baskets, finishing PTA phone calls, sorting the mail.

■ Make "having fun" a top priority on your things-to-do list. Because Judging mothers tend to think "I'll relax as soon as my work is finished," they seldom get to it because, when it comes to mothering, the work is never done. Be sure to build in to your schedule some time off — at least 30 minutes a day — not tied to finishing a job. Talk to a favorite friend, take a spring walk, or read the newspaper.

■ Find new ways to have fun with your children. Many Judging mothers worry that they don't enjoy time with their children as much as they think they "should" or as much as they'd like to. Try taking your children out of the house — so you're not distracted by what needs to be done at home. Or introduce your child to what was fun for you when you were your child's age. Particularly with young children, it's easier for them to "play" at what's fun for you than for you to "play" at what's fun for them. And remember, real fun won't happen on schedule, regularly, day after day.

■ Try to balance your need for order with other family members' lower needs for order. You might find ways to contain their disorder so you can function well without forcing loved ones to meet your standards all the time. Try a closed-door, clear-path policy: "Your room can be as messy as you'd like as long as the common areas are neat and there's a clear path between the bed and door."

■ Adopt a weekend-off policy — "Monday through Friday we'll stick to my plan, Saturday and Sunday we'll keep open."

■ Allow yourself to take pleasure in straightening the house. Think of it as therapeutic, not a job. As "un-fun" as that sounds, Judging mothers often say they enjoy setting the house in order. If you have young children, consider hiring a sitter so you can clean your house uninterrupted, or send them to Grandma's so you can straighten up.

*The Judging mother is generally willing to call the shots when she believes being directive is in her children's best interests. She may decide she needs to establish a "no cookies after 4 p.m." rule to make sure they eat a good dinner.*

## *The Perceiving Mother*

### MAY GRAVITATE TOWARD . . .

■ Being tolerant and accepting, letting her children be themselves without pushing or shaping

■ Being spontaneous; enjoying "hanging out" with her children

■ Being responsive to a child's interruptions

■ Staying open-minded while listening to her children

■ Exposing her children to a variety of experiences and people — emphasizing exploration, discovery, curiosity — getting children to experience everything they can

■ Letting her children make many of their own choices; being willing to follow their lead

■ Being relaxed about children's clutter, disorder, chaos — if they are having fun

■ Being easy-going and relaxed when milk spills, plans get upset, or children misbehave

### THE **PERCEIVING** MOTHER MAY STRUGGLE WITH . . .

■ Keeping her household organized and in order, doing chores on a regular basis

■ Keeping her children on task and on time — getting out the door in the morning for school, getting them to bed, ensuring homework is done

**A** *Perceiving mother couldn't understand her Judging teenage daughter's irritation over dinner not being served on time. "Learning type, I began to suspect the source of our problem," says the mother. "To me, anytime I served dinner between 5:30 and 8:30, it was 'on time.' To her, 'on time' meant between 6:15 and 6:30. We've compromised. 'On time' for both of us now means between 6 and 7."*

■ Not leaving things until the last minute or letting things go too far

■ Not taking on way too much

■ Living with daily routines and everyday sameness

■ Juggling everyone's schedule, even though her children's exposure to experiences is a priority

■ Setting limits for her children, being consistent, and following through

■ Staying focused on finishing a task

■ Providing the structured environment a Judging child may need to feel secure

## TIPS FOR THE **PERCEIVING** MOTHER

*"Taking care of me" means freedom
from a tight schedule.*

■ Allow yourself at least one slow, unscheduled morning on the weekend to "hang out" and recover from the busy week. You might consider taking a summer off from schedules.

■ Start your day with a crisis list rather than a things-to-do list. Write down one to three things you must do or everything will fall apart — "get bread and milk, call the plumber, take Sue for a check-up" — and post it on the refrigerator. Keeping the list to the "essentials" may help you stay focused and flexible to handle what the day brings.

■ Don't back yourself into a corner with a lot of rules you'll ultimately find too restrictive. Perceiving mothers usually function better with a few basic intents or ideals. Instead of a "no doughnuts, pancakes, or waffles for breakfast" rule, you may have more success posting a sign which says "make healthy food choices when you eat a meal or snack."

■ Give yourself some breathing room when making plans, particularly when you're dealing with Judgers. Judgers hear Perceivers coming to "firm" decisions even when Perceivers are still keeping their options open. If plans change, the Judgers feel let down, that they can't count on Perceivers to follow through. Be clear about what you can commit to while providing Judgers with plans and structure. Say "I'll be home for dinner between 5:30 and 6:30" instead of "I'll be home at 6." Then when you show up at 6:15, you'll be considered on time.

■ Remember that although you're drawn to many experiences for your children, each organized activity involves structure, scheduling, planning, and focus on your part. Limit your children to one structured activity a week that you're responsible for. Let the rest of your child's experiences be spontaneous and unstructured. Yes, your child can participate in swimming, dance, basketball, choir ... but consecutively, not concurrently.

*Illustration from Parenting Style Slide Set*

*Tolerant and accepting, the Perceiving mother can let children develop at their own pace. Even a kindergartner who still enjoys a pacifier may not phase her. "Who's it hurting?" she reasons. "She'll give it up when she's ready."*

# PART FOUR

# MOTHERING PROFILES

# OF THE 16 TYPES

## YOU'RE UNIQUE!

Your preference in each of the four categories determines your personality type. There are 16 possible combinations — 16 different personality types.

According to Jungian type theory, each of the 16 personality types has its own unique dynamics. It is not simply a matter of adding up the characteristics of the four preferences that make up your individual type.

The total is more than the sum of the parts. For example, an ISFJ is more than the descriptions for Introversion, Sensing, Feeling, and Judging. When any four preferences combine into a personality type, there is a dynamic interaction. Each combination creates its own essence, something that makes that type different than any other personality type. Changing even one preference changes that essence.

In short, each of the 16 type mothers is unique. M.O.M.S. research revealed that each type mother had a special gift for her children — something she does effortlessly and better than any other type mother — indeed, something that makes her children lucky to have her as a mother. Each profile tries to capture that essence and provide additional strengths, struggles, and personalized mother-to-mother tips.

The descriptions in this section are based on in-depth interviews with mothers of all 16 personality types. As much as possible, the descriptions make use of the women's own words to describe themselves. Yes, each type mother has a language all her own! You'll notice many quotations throughout.

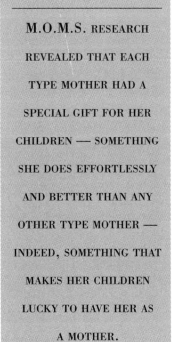

M.O.M.S. RESEARCH REVEALED THAT EACH TYPE MOTHER HAD A SPECIAL GIFT FOR HER CHILDREN — SOMETHING SHE DOES EFFORTLESSLY AND BETTER THAN ANY OTHER TYPE MOTHER — INDEED, SOMETHING THAT MAKES HER CHILDREN LUCKY TO HAVE HER AS A MOTHER.

## YOUR PERSONALITY CORE

This section organizes the 16 personality types by the middle two letters in the type. That is, all four ST types are grouped together, all SFs, all NFs, and all NTs. Many experts identify the middle two letters of your type as your "personality core." If you share the middle two letters with someone else, you are likely to think that person is "on your same wavelength" or a "kindred spirit." M.O.M.S. research indicated that, when it comes to mothering, women who share a personality core tend to "see" things the same way, share many values, and take a similar approach to mothering.

And what about the first and last letters of your type: EJ, EP, IJ, or IP? Some experts refer to them as the "living differences" — how you like to live with others on a day-to-day basis. For example, these preferences determine the amount of verbal interacting you prefer and how orderly you like your common living space.

When it comes to mothering, the "living differences" influence the way you express your personality core everyday.

## FINDING YOUR PROFILE

At this point, if you are certain of your personality type, the M.O.M.S. description of you as a mother should ring true ... and offer new insights that will improve your mothering satisfaction.

After you've found your own profile, you may want to search for your mother's, your sister's, or your best friend's. Please, don't feel compelled to read the 16 type descriptions from beginning to end. That would be mind boggling (especially when your head is already full of children!).

If, however, you're uncertain as to what your personality type is, be assured: you're in good company. It is not uncommon for people in the early stages of learning about personality type to be considering one, two, or even three possibilities.

M.O.M.S. research indicates mothers in particular may be confused. Because motherhood is a transforming experience — we are stretched and become competent in so many different areas — your true preferences may elude you.

For those who are still searching for the "real me," you can use Part Four to try to figure out who you are by reading several descriptions of personality types. Hopefully, one of these profiles will leap out and say "that's me, all right!"

Or you may end up still thinking you're half this and half that. And that's okay too. As well-developed and helpful as this framework of personality type is, no one theory can explain everything about you.

Just take what is helpful from this handbook and don't worry about the rest.

*An INFJ mother and her ESTP son like to visit with each other at the end of the day before going to bed. But they've established some important procedures to ensure they each get their needs met. After the mother has put her ENFP daughter to bed, she takes 30 to 45 minutes of quiet time alone in her room to recharge; the son reads in his room. Then she comes to his room for a visit. "Visiting" to the NF mother means sharing feelings, talking about relationships, and finding out how things are going with friends and at school. To the ST son, "visiting" means problem-solving, answering math questions, and challenging his intellect and knowledge of facts. To accommodate both sets of needs, the mother might ask her son to rank his friends or teachers on the basis of how well he likes them; he must also give the reasons why. This routine also provides structure for the IJ mother for dealing with an EP son who would like to talk whenever he gets the urge.*

# ISTJ

## *The "Responsibility" Mother*

The ISTJ mother has a highly developed sense of responsibility: for work, home, family ... particularly her children. Whether she's overseeing daily baths or insisting on a 10 p.m. curfew, her efforts are largely focused on providing her children with order and routine. She wants them, regardless of age, to be able to count on her and the structure she provides.

In carrying out her commitment to her responsibilities, the ISTJ mother is organized, industrious, and detail-oriented. Because her focus is the day-to-day realities of life, her children are likely to feel secure and well provided for.

The ISTJ mother also sets a good example and provides her children with practical guidance on being a productive, responsible individual. Still, with all her seriousness, she may delight family members with her quick wit and observations about the details of life.

### STRENGTHS

■ *Providing for her children's practical needs.* The ISTJ mother tends to her children's basic needs on a day-to-day routine, seeing to it they're healthy, well fed, clean, warm, and well rested.

■ *Providing security.* For the ISTJ mother, children thrive in a family structure where roles and boundaries are well defined. She makes it clear: Parents are parents, children are children.

■ *Preparing her children for life in the real world.* The ISTJ mother believes children must ultimately be independent and on their own. Her goal is to instill good study habits and show them "how to be organized" and make effective use of time. She also views it as her responsibility to discuss the pros and cons of different ways people earn a living.

> 'I HAVE A SERIOUS LOVE AFFAIR WITH TO-DO LISTS. I COULD SIT FOR HOURS READING, ORGANIZING, AND REARRANGING MY WEEKLY CALENDAR.'

■ *Teaching her children how to work hard.* The ISTJ mother encourages her children to do for themselves. Not only does she set the standard for hard work, she gives them responsibility for specific "jobs" around the house, expects them to do their best at school, and insists they clean up after themselves.

### STRUGGLES

■ *Flexibility.* If structure is her byword, the ISTJ mother may struggle most with being adaptable. Little children are spontaneous and unpredictable, older children have minds of their own, and letting children invite friends into the home can leave her feeling there's no order in her life.

■ *Being hard on herself.* Aware of all that needs to be done, the ISTJ mother may be a perfectionist who wants things done right and on time. Proceeding at an intense pace, she may find it difficult to relax until all her work is done.

■ *Exhaustion.* Private and inwardly focused, the ISTJ mother may find herself constantly drained by disorder and children's commotion. She may feel overwhelmed, unable to maintain order or struggling to find any time alone to recharge.

### TIPS

■ The best gift an ISTJ mother can give herself is uninterrupted quiet time each day. She may need to have someone take her children to the park each afternoon or turn off the phone to savor the stillness during the hours they're at school or at a friend's. She may choose to spend her private time setting things in order or getting caught up.

■ Because she needs structure to relax fully, the ISTJ mother may need to plan regular times that are okay to let down, knowing it won't disrupt the entire day. If her family can help finish what she needs to complete before relaxing, everyone may benefit.

# ESTP

## *The "Action Adventure" Mother*

Active and spontaneous, the ESTP mother can turn ordinary life into a fun-filled adventure. She makes dull routines exciting and chores a "let's do it again" kind of game. Her best times are those spent with her children actively doing, particularly if it's spur of the moment, innovative, and unconventional.

Full of energy and enthusiasm for living in the moment, the ESTP mother gives her children every opportunity to experience all that life has to offer — touching, seeing, moving, doing ... and people. She's interested in stimulating their senses so they can take life in and live it.

The ESTP mother is matter-of-fact — "what you see is what you get." She mothers without hidden agendas and takes life and people as they are. Her children know where they stand. She is able to develop a close relationship with them based on honesty and a strong family orientation as well as sharing a wide variety of experiences.

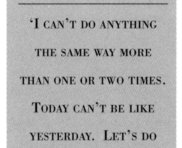

'I CAN'T DO ANYTHING THE SAME WAY MORE THAN ONE OR TWO TIMES. TODAY CAN'T BE LIKE YESTERDAY. LET'S DO SOMETHING DIFFERENT!'

### STRENGTHS

■ *Making the ordinary exciting.* The ESTP mother is a whiz at creating fun, turning "boring" aspects of day-to-day living into interesting things to do. She may detest making dinner at a scheduled time each day but thoroughly enjoy spending a Saturday with all family members up to their elbows in flour and laughter making homemade ravioli.

■ *Encouraging her children to explore the world.* Classes, outings, travel, sports teams, mud puddles, friends — all are to be experienced and enjoyed ... and used as opportunities for a child to discover and develop his or her strengths and special interests.

■ *Doing and going with her children ... on their level.* Action-oriented and constantly on the go, the ESTP mother gets actively involved in what her children are doing. She doesn't just sign them up for football, she goes out and tosses the football with them. She doesn't just listen to their newest CD, she joins in and imitates the rock star.

■ *Flexibility.* Easy going and straightforward, the ESTP mother is content to go with the flow and rarely loses her cool. In fact, she thrives on "chaos" and lives a no-strings-attached lifestyle.

### STRUGGLES

■ *Routine.* The ESTP mother struggles with household routines: organizing children every morning for school, keeping shopping lists, straightening the house on a regular basis, and cooking dinner every night. Doing the same things the same way day after day may be what some children need to feel secure, but it requires intense effort for the ESTP.

■ *Being still.* The ESTP mother struggles with the quiet and slow times of family life — sitting down to talk or read with a child one-on-one.

■ *Maintaining focus.* The ESTP mother may struggle to see a household task or other routine project through from start to finish. Easily distracted, she will likely drop everything when something else captures her attention.

### TIPS

■ The ESTP needs a repertoire of activities that balance her need for action and spontaneity with a child's need for downtime. Having intimate talks while walking in the woods or driving around in the car may meet her need for "going" while responding to a child's need for quiet togetherness.

■ The greatest gift the ESTP can give herself is acceptance of her mothering gifts. She needs to stop comparing herself to the "other" mothers — the ones who seem to keep a smooth-running household, have dinner on the table at 6 p.m. every night, and do laundry on Mondays. The ESTP mother may feel out of step with this more domestic mother, but her love of action and spontaneity make her very much in tune with children everywhere.

# ISTP

## *The "Give 'Em Their Space" Mother*

Nonintrusive and respectful of differences, the ISTP mother gives her children the personal space they need to develop as separate, self-sufficient individuals. As children grow and mature, she enjoys observing how each one becomes his or her own person. She seeks to accept and honor each one's interests, opinions, and choices.

The ISTP mother does not believe in authority or control for its own sake. Instead, she favors a non-directive approach. Yet she has high expectations for each child's self-discipline ... as a key to self sufficiency.

To these ends, the ISTP mother wants to "be there" for her children — to meet their basic needs and keep them safe. Her goal is to help her children think for themselves and take responsibility for their own actions.

### STRENGTHS

■ *Honoring differences.* While she may not always agree with them, the ISTP mother fundamentally believes her children have the right to their own points of view. She tends to follow their lead in what interests them, rather than trying to shape or control what or how they think.

■ *Respecting a child's privacy.* The ISTP mother provides her children with the physical and emotional privacy she values for herself. She is careful to knock before entering a child's room, doesn't ask who called on the phone, and backs off from asking personal questions that to her seem intrusive.

■ *Fostering self-sufficiency.* The ISTP mother believes in self-discipline. Not liking to be confined by rules or authority herself, she may be intentionally "lenient" with her children so they can think situations through on their own, choose their actions, and then assess their own behavior.

■ *Engaging children in intellectual discussions.* As she helps her children think for themselves, the ISTP mother enjoys intellectual discussions with them at any age. Her best times as a mother may be those

moments when she and her children discuss what they are studying at school — grammar, geography, world events — or what they want to do in life.

### STRUGGLES

■ *Providing emotional support.* The ISTP mother may feel out of her element when it comes to giving a child the emotional closeness he or she needs. She may struggle with showing warmth and affection, coaxing a scared child, or figuring out the emotional aspects of a child's behavior.

■ *Asking personal questions.* When her child needs help handling an emotional issue, the ISTP mother may be reluctant to probe his or her feelings — she doesn't want to put the child on the spot or set off an emotional outburst. But her children may confuse her nonintrusive behavior with not caring.

> 'MY FEELINGS ARE MY OWN BUSINESS. NOT THEIRS. SO I HONOR *THEIR* PRIVACY TOO.'

■ *Traditional domestic tasks.* Handling the domestic side of child-raising does not appeal to the ISTP mother. She tends to be uncomfortable if called on to fix home-cooked meals regularly, insist children sit down to eat, dress them in matching outfits, or provide little touches that make their rooms homey.

### TIPS

■ The ISTP needs to find a comfortable way to connect with her children's feelings and concerns on a regular basis. She can develop systems or techniques the family can use to initiate more personal conversations. For example, a child might place a baseball cap on his door handle by 7 p.m. as a signal to his mother that he would appreciate a bedtime chat that night. Or she might keep an open mother-daughter journal that allows for each one to communicate personal thoughts through written conversation.

■ The greatest gift the ISTP mother can give herself is a break from day-to-day household routines. She may enjoy going out by herself to visit a bookstore or see a movie. Or she may prefer to hire a housekeeper (if she can afford it), or delegate those chores she finds intolerable to other family members.

# ESTJ

## *The "How To" Mother*

Organized and comfortable being in charge, the ESTJ mother knows "how to" get things done, make things happen, and accomplish much on behalf of her children. Whether she is encouraging them to get involved in organized activities or talking with them about their personal concerns, children of the ESTJ mother learn "how to" succeed in life.

Upbeat and matter-of-fact, the ESTJ mother is intent on her children having the best. She puts her skills and talents to work to this end, from planning trips that supplement their studies to raising funds for new playground equipment. She is happiest when her efforts produce concrete results — children who try out for teams, participate in academic competitions, or are leaders among their peers.

The ESTJ mother runs a tight household. She is apt to have predictable expectations, consistent routines, standard procedures, and well-defined boundaries, all of which help her children feel protected and secure.

> 'WE'RE THE MOTHERS YOU LIKE TO CARPOOL WITH. NOT ONLY ARE WE ON TIME, WE ORGANIZE THE DRIVING SCHEDULE FOR EVERYONE.'

### STRENGTHS

■ *Organization and planning.* The ESTJ mother is naturally suited to managing a busy, active family. She can juggle many tasks and get a lot done. Her children know they can depend on her to follow through and take care of their basic needs.

■ *Teaching children practical skills for success.* The ESTJ mother knows what it takes to succeed — do your work before you play, don't burn bridges, look adults in the eye when you shake hands, make new friends but keep the old, plan ahead for deadlines, organize your time.

■ *Teaching children how to problem-solve.* The ESTJ mother loves talking to her children about what's on their minds. She uses their issues and concerns as "teaching moments" to help them with their problem-solving, whether it's handling a school assignment or managing trouble with friends.

■ *Social adeptness and people orientation.* By word and example, the ESTJ mother teaches her children the joys and skills of moving comfortably among people and groups. She does what she can to create a network of friends, extended family, and community organizations for her children.

### STRUGGLES

■ *Sense of self.* The ESTJ mother often feels overly responsible for her children's successes and failures. She may find herself living through their successes or using their behavior to measure her competence as a mother.

■ *Letting go.* The ESTJ mother struggles to let children of all ages do things their own way. When her children are young, she may be frustrated that she can't *make* them eat vegetables or fall asleep on schedule. As they get older, she may stay involved, at risk of "trying to run their lives."

■ *Acceptance.* The ESTJ mother may struggle to accept each child just the way he or she is. Because she has a picture of what would be best for each one, her children may feel that anything short of her idea of perfection isn't good enough.

### TIPS

■ The ESTJ mother needs opportunities to feel competent separate from the job of mothering. Getting feedback for her ability to manage projects — both paid and volunteer — can provide objective measures of her competence.

■ The ESTJ mother needs a place where she can exercise her need for structure or a project that is "totally under control." If she can claim such a place or project, she may find it easier to be more flexible and spontaneous when it's called for.

# ISFJ

## *The "Tender Loving Care" Mother*

Gentle and kind, the ISFJ mother provides her children with generous amounts of tenderness, affection, and the comfort of daily routine. Her aim is to "be there" for her children, physically and emotionally. She is sensitive to their feelings, offering closeness, understanding, and quiet support.

Loyal and devoted, the ISFJ mother has a strong sense of duty and consistently puts her children's needs first. She delights in taking care of the little things that matter to a child, making each one feel loved and special.

To provide her family with security and warmth, the ISFJ mother tends to the practical and domestic, aiming for a smooth-running household and an attractive home. She also observes and conveys the value and importance of family traditions.

### STRENGTHS

■ *Showing love in practical ways.* The ISFJ mother shows her love with home-cooked meals, an orderly house, neatly folded laundry, hand-made holiday decorations ... and time with each child in quiet togetherness.

■ *Tending to the little things.* The ISFJ mother goes the extra mile to take care of what's important in a child's life — from the child's point of view. Whether it's searching for hours for a lost toy, reading a favorite bed-time story for the 51st time, or volunteering as a teacher's helper in her child's classroom, the ISFJ knows what matters to her child and comes through.

■ *Establishing boundaries.* The ISFJ mother provides a secure environment for her family by defining clear roles for parent and child, steady and consistent rules, and predictable routines. Her children know what they can count on.

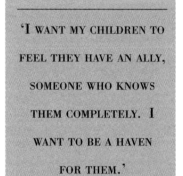

'I WANT MY CHILDREN TO FEEL THEY HAVE AN ALLY, SOMEONE WHO KNOWS THEM COMPLETELY. I WANT TO BE A HAVEN FOR THEM.'

■ *Sensitivity.* Loving and kind, the ISFJ mother is a patient listener, valuing and respecting each child's feelings and concerns.

### STRUGGLES

■ *Appreciation.* Because she serves behind the scenes and makes household and mothering tasks look effortless, the ISFJ may struggle with feeling taken for granted. She may feel hurt if loved ones fail to notice or appreciate her efforts.

■ *Guilt.* With a fierce sense of being duty-bound to family, home, and other commitments she has made, the ISFJ is vulnerable to both internal and external "shoulds" and feelings of guilt.

■ *Fear of being a 'wet blanket.'* The ISFJ, knowing she pours herself into her family and has a high need for order and structure, wonders about the impact she has on her loved ones. She may worry that her children find her too serious, overly sensible, or stifling.

### TIPS

■ The ISFJ mother can benefit from cultivating her own interests and putting her needs first every so often. Young children may appreciate her unwavering attention. But older children with increasing needs for independence may find it burdensome. Encouraging herself to experience life beyond the responsibilities of motherhood can give the ISFJ perspective and a sense of fun and joyful living her family is sure to appreciate.

■ Because she needs structure and quiet to fully relax, the ISFJ mother may need to schedule time off on a regular basis — a half hour alone each day, one night a week when she doesn't prepare the meal, a monthly outing by herself, a regular manicure appointment, or a daily walk in the fresh air.

# E S F P

## *The "Totally There" Mother*

Energetic and people-oriented, the ESFP mother lives in the moment, "totally there" for her children — totally focused on them when she is with them. She enjoys being with her children and can respond to their needs "on the spot," ensuring that they feel loved and cared for.

Fun-loving, friendly, and outgoing, the ESFP mother actively engages her children in a wide variety of experiences. They can count on her to strike up a conversation with a fellow shopper at the market or with the bus driver, introducing them to the joys of people everywhere.

Devoted and practical, the ESFP mother also enjoys doing for her children. She is attentive to their feelings and is deeply touched by every joy or hurt they experience.

### STRENGTHS

■ *Being there.* The ESFP mother may consider herself 100% devoted to her children. As such, her first priority is "being there" for them whenever they need her — being on call 24 hours a day, showering them with unconditional love, comforting them when they hurt.

■ *Playfulness.* Child-oriented and filled with joy for living, the ESFP mother knows how to have fun and laugh with her children, perhaps acting like a kid again herself. She delights in having children around, and that includes other people's children. Her house may be the neighborhood hang-out.

■ *Family focus.* A proponent of family closeness and unity, the ESFP mother seeks to instill a strong sense of family in her children. She encourages everyone to spend time together and wants her children to know that family comes first ... that family members support each other through thick and thin.

'I LIKE TO GIVE MY CHILDREN AN IMMEDIATE RESPONSE. IT'S NOT LIKE THERE'S ONE TIME FOR HUGS AND ANOTHER TO MAKE SANDWICHES.'

■ *Flexibility.* Unstructured and non-restrictive, the ESFP mother is spontaneous. She enjoys going with the flow of children of all ages.

### STRUGGLES

■ *Discipline.* Although well-behaved children are a high priority for her, the ESFP mother may not feel confident as a disciplinarian. Struggling to gain an objective point of view, she may wonder, "Should I make an issue of this or let it go this one time?" If she is confronted with a situation where her actions could make a child unhappy, she may think setting limits is "mean." And sticking to limits over the long run may be harder for her than for her child.

■ *Letting go.* Encouraging independence in her children can be difficult for the ESFP mother. Backing off goes against her natural inclination to get involved, be close, and do things for them.

■ *When her children are hurt.* The ESFP mother may become overly upset when her children's feelings are hurt or when they're facing life's hard knocks. She may need steady reassurance that they'll be okay.

### TIPS

■ The ESFP mother can benefit from joining a group of mothers who have children the same age as hers. Together these women can point out different perspectives, options, and ways of doing things, as well as affirm that "she's not the only one." Supporting one another in their mothering can help provide the objectivity and reassurance she needs.

■ The ESFP mother needs to remember to tune in to her needs and put them first once in a while. Always giving and being "totally there" for her children, she may burn-out and have nothing left for herself, which can leave her feeling resentful and angry. The added benefit of putting the focus on herself: the ESFP gives her children space and time to develop their independence.

# ISFP

## *The "Giving" Mother*

Quiet and unassuming in her devotion, the ISFP mother is responsive to her children's needs, offering behind-the-scenes love and support. She is gentle and nonintrusive, flexible and adaptable.

A "be there" mother, the ISFP takes pleasure in physically caring for her children and doing for them. Her best times might be "doing little things" with each child one-on-one.

More than anything, the ISFP mother wants her children to know they are loved. And she enjoys being needed in return.

Dedicated to raising children who are responsible and care for others, she favors a non-directive approach: instilling values by setting a good example. She may be a strong role model for community service.

### STRENGTHS

■ *Accessibility and flexibility.* The ISFP mother is available to her children. Because she can readily "go with the flow," the ISFP is well suited to meeting the unpredictable needs of small children. Adult children of ISFPs say they always knew they were loved and accepted growing up — mom was never too busy to spend time together, give a hug, work a puzzle, or help with homework.

■ *Her personal touch.* The ISFP mother is responsive to each child, tending to the needs of the moment. When one is sick, she makes jello, and when he wants to learn to ride his bike, she runs along holding the seat. She'll work with another child on a puzzle or bake favorite cookies. The ISFP likes doing the little things that matter most to her children.

■ *Providing gentle support.* Sympathetic and comforting, the ISFP mother soothes a child's upset feelings with physical closeness and quiet talk. She is reassuring and encouraging, helping her children believe they can do anything they want.

■ *Teaching by example.* To impart the values she holds most dear, the ISFP mother does not preach, force, or push her children. She believes children learn best by the example set for them; if her children see her do a good deed, they will learn to do it

> 'A PEOPLE PLEASER FROM DAY ONE, IT TOOK ME 30 YEARS TO FIGURE OUT I COULD SAY "NO."'

as well. She strives to set a good example of a life of service to family, friends, and community, and to care for all living creatures.

### STRUGGLES

■ *Selflessness.* Because she is generous and a "people pleaser," the ISFP mother may struggle with giving too much of herself. As a result, she may not know her own interests and needs. She may also become burned-out and angry with loved ones asking so much of her.

■ *Assertiveness.* As she naturally adapts to the needs and wants of others, the ISFP mother may find it extremely hard to stand up for herself and say "no." She may also have difficulty asking for help ... even when it's in everyone's best interest. She may struggle most to assert herself with traditional authority figures, such as teachers and medical professionals.

■ *Routine and productivity.* Organizing and keeping daily family routines can seem overwhelming to the ISFP mother, whether her task is overseeing homework, getting children to school on time, or preparing meals. Sporadic in her focus, she tends to procrastinate; she often feels unproductive, wondering at times how other mothers accomplish so much.

### TIPS

■ The greatest gift the ISFP mother can give herself is a break from constantly giving to her children — and give to herself instead. Long blocks of time alone to read, watch a movie, or putter around the house are well deserved. And outside interests can give her perspective. By putting the focus on herself once in a while, the ISFP mother is actually giving to her children as well: they have time and space for their own needs, and she's setting a good example of how one takes care of oneself.

■ The ISFP mother may benefit from outside support in learning how to say "no" and assert herself. A supportive partner, good friend, or professional counselor may be able to model new approaches, offer insight, and encourage her to stand up for herself more.

# ESFJ

## *The "Happy Together" Mother*

The ESFJ mother has a highly developed sense of family and what it takes to be happy in life. Capable and personally invested, she strives to create a happy family where togetherness and harmony flourish. Whether it's taking her children to the park or putting on a holiday feast, her efforts are directed toward having everyone be "happy together."

To many, the ESFJ personifies motherhood. She promotes traditional values, tends to the practical and domestic, provides the family with order and structure, and is directly involved with her children's day-to-day living. The ESFJ mother is a "doer," and she's never happier than when she's "doing" for her family.

Believing the home is central to family life, the ESFJ mother excels at creating an atmosphere that is attractive and offers security.

Energetic and people-oriented, she is drawn to community and the social scene. She helps her children discover the joys of people and groups.

### STRENGTHS

■ *Cultivating close relationships with her children.* The ESFJ mother is devoted to taking care of her children's needs, physical and emotional. She is especially sensitive to their feelings, offering personal warmth, comfort, and plenty of "I love yous."

■ *Making people connections with the larger world.* Sociable and friendly, the ESFJ mother provides her children with opportunities and activities to connect with community and friends as well as family, often serving as the family's "social director."

■ *Sharing practical wisdom.* The ESFJ mother wants her children to know how to get along in the world. She values what is "appropriate" and teaches her children the right things to do and say in a wide variety of situations.

> 'I LIKE IT WHEN MY CHILDREN ARE HAPPY ON THEIR OWN, BUT I LOVE IT WHEN THE WHOLE FAMILY IS HAPPY TOGETHER.'

■ *Providing a home base.* The ESFJ mother creates a home atmosphere that can serve as an anchor in the storm for her children. Home to her is also the place for informal gatherings and special events, such as family birthdays and holidays. A gracious hostess, she extends the warmth and hospitality of her home to family and friends.

### STRUGGLES

■ *Family disharmony.* The ESFJ mother gladly puts forth effort to orchestrate good times for the whole family together. She can feel frustrated, annoyed, and hurt, however, when family members are fighting, someone is hurt, or some don't want to participate.

■ *Judgment and control.* The ESFJ mother has a good idea of what she wants for her child, and she worries when her child chooses a path different from the one she has envisioned. She may struggle to understand and accept a child who is different, finding it difficult to back off and let go.

■ *Perfectionism.* In an effort to get everything done right and on time, the ESFJ mother is prone to overfunctioning. The stress may lead her to nit-pick or over-focus on details to make everything perfect.

### TIPS

■ When her children are squabbling, the ESFJ mother needs to remind herself that healthy relationships require a certain amount of conflict and "clearing the air" to grow and flourish. Allowing family members to work out differences on their own can sometimes be the best way to promote the close, harmonious relationships she wants for her family over the long run.

■ Driven by a lot of "shoulds," the ESFJ mother is susceptible to others' judgments and the desire to please, not to mention her own perfectionism. She may have a hard time relaxing. The greatest gift the ESFJ mother can give herself is enforced regular breaks from the intensity of family life and constantly giving and doing for others. A little relaxation and fun need to be put at the top of her to-do list everyday.

# INFJ

## *The "Know Thyself" Mother*

Sensitive and family-focused, the INFJ mother looks for and encourages the unique potential of each child. Self-knowledge may be her byword. Her aim is to help each child develop a sense of identity and cultivate personal growth. In fact, she may value the mothering experience as a catalyst to her own personal growth and self-knowledge.

The INFJ mother spends time observing and understanding each child. She is drawn to intimate conversations and seeks a free exchange of feelings and thoughts.

Sympathetic and accommodating, the INFJ mother strives to meet the important yet sometimes conflicting needs of each family member in harmonious and creative ways.

She is conscientious and intense as well. Probably no one takes life and child-raising more seriously than the INFJ. She approaches mothering as a profession requiring her best self.

> 'I BELIEVE THE JOY OF MOTHERHOOD IS SELF-DISCOVERY — FOR THEM AND FOR ME.'

### STRENGTHS

■ *Connecting one-on-one with each child.* The INFJ mother listens, observes, and reflects to develop an understanding of who each child really is. She "knows" her child and desires a close relationship. She connects and keeps in touch with each child as a unique individual.

■ *Providing her children with emotional support.* The INFJ mother is sensitive to her children's feelings, not shying away from helping them deal with even their heaviest emotions. She seeks to smooth out the rough edges of their experiences with a comforting presence and her broader perspectives.

■ *Profundity.* Focused on understanding values, spirituality, culture, and society, the INFJ mother provides awareness and insights into the subtleties and lessons of life beyond a child's immediate experience and questions.

■ *Creativity.* The INFJ mother can dream up unusual, fun projects her children can do to occupy their time and enrich their day-to-day experience, such as fantasy games to play, theme parties, or special snacks to make from healthy foods.

### STRUGGLES

■ *Details.* The INFJ mother may gravitate toward the idea of getting the family and household organized and in order, only to exhaust herself with nitty-gritty follow-through. Regular baths for small children, weekly laundry, daily meals, picking up clutter, and ongoing repairs can be overwhelming.

■ *Real life vs. the ideal.* Because she lives with an ideal in her mind, the INFJ mother often has unrealistic expectations of herself and others. She may feel inadequate and critical of herself when reality falls short of her ideal.

■ *Giving too much.* The INFJ mother may be prone to over-accommodation and self-sacrifice as a way to maintain family harmony. She struggles with the ramifications: a child who is too dependent and a mother who is depleted and resentful.

### TIPS

■ Although she is drawn to people, the INFJ mother must remember that she needs time alone on a regular basis. Since her children are greatly affected by her mood swings, she is also giving to her children when she accommodates her Introversion. Time alone to meditate, journal, listen to music, and enjoy nature as well as intimate discussions with close friends can do wonders to bring peace to herself. For the INFJ especially, "If Mom ain't okay, ain't nobody okay."

■ The INFJ mother needs to try to take life less seriously ... to lighten up and take time to look at what life "is" rather than try to make it what it "should be." By living in the moment rather than the future, she can also help curb her tendency to take an isolated fact and extrapolate a catastrophic outcome.

# ENFP

## *The "Kids R Fun" Mother*

Playful and energetic, the ENFP mother finds her children to be good company and enjoys being with them. In fact, she says being with children justifies her own "being a kid again." And children say she's fun to be with — spontaneous, hearty, and imaginative.

Naturally drawn to introducing her children to the joys of life, the ENFP is something of a free spirit. She is less concerned with rules, routines, and schedules, and more inclined to give her children plenty of free time to play, explore on their own or with her, and have fun together.

Tuned in to her children, the ENFP mother enthusiastically encourages each one's individuality and unique potential through a great variety of experiences. She is also quick to identify with others' feelings and thoughts, making her an empathetic supporter of her children ... not to mention her mate and many, many friends.

### STRENGTHS

■ *Playfulness.* The ENFP mother provides her children with delightful companionship. Comfortable playing at their level, she may enjoy dancing on the table, jumping rope in the house, or doing somersaults in the swimming pool. She is equally happy "hanging out," watching a movie, or window shopping ... as long as everyone is having fun together.

■ *Helping a child identify and cultivate his or her gifts.* Perceptive and people-smart, the ENFP mother helps her children recognize their talents. Enthusiastically, she helps each one develop his or her unique potential — she provides experiences and opportunities that expand a child's interests and offers her ongoing encouragement and support.

■ *Sensitivity and empathy.* The ENFP mother is aware of her children — what they're feeling and what's going on in their lives. Drawn to the pleasures of conversation and adept at heart-to-heart talks, she listens to them empathetically without judging.

> 'WHATEVER I ENJOY — PLAYING TAG OR SINGING IN THE CAR — I CAN DO IT WITH KIDS AROUND. AND IT'S TOTALLY LEGITIMATE!'

■ *Flexibility.* Despite the confusion of a busy, fast-paced lifestyle and concurrent family activities, the ENFP mother can usually stay calm and go with the flow. She is rarely flustered by a change of plans, a spilled glass of milk, or last-minute requests.

### STRUGGLES

■ *Maintaining emotional boundaries.* When one of her children is having a difficult time, the ENFP mother may struggle to maintain a helpful emotional distance. She may over-identify with a child's concerns, aching with his or her every hurt, exaggerating its importance, and ultimately needing reassurance from the child that he or she will be okay.

■ *Details.* The ENFP mother struggles with the details, organization, and routines of day-to-day living. Being "on time," remembering permission slips, regular mealtimes, and laundry can drive her to distraction. She may let mundane chores turn into mini-crises, because she enjoys the rush.

■ *Firmness.* Worried about making a bad decision or taking a wrong course of action, the ENFP mother may find it difficult to be objective, decisive, and firm-minded, when appropriate. Teenagers especially may find her indulgent and inconsistent.

### TIPS

■ When dealing with her children's personal concerns, the ENFP mother needs to step back and ask herself, "Whose problem is this anyway?" and "Is this really that terrible?" To keep from overfunctioning, she might enlist the help and support of a Thinking-Judging spouse or friend who can give her a more objective perspective.

■ Because she is naturally drawn to a variety of activities and tending to family members' emotional well-being, the ENFP mother can easily burn-out. She may find it hard to relax; however, 15-minute catnaps, physical exercise, and long walks can keep her energized. Four-handkerchief movies, sad books, and pouring out her heart to a close friend can help her release her emotional stress.

# INFP

## *The "Tuned In" Mother*

Aware, astute, and understanding, the INFP mother is sensitive to her child's needs, feelings, and perceptions. By observing and listening to the cues of the whole child, she is "tuned in" and naturally develops an intuitive feel for what he or she needs. Responsive and helpful as well, she tends patiently to those needs as they arise.

The INFP mother is comfortable letting her children follow their own course of development and make their own choices. She offers encouragement and uses her insights to head off trouble and difficult issues.

The INFP mother takes vicarious pleasure giving her children good experiences and watching them enjoy childhood. She's happiest creating pleasant, memorable times for the whole family.

## STRENGTHS

■ *Cultivating a one-on-one relationship with each child.* Accepting and gentle, the INFP mother places a high value on having a close relationship with each child. In cultivating that relationship, she readily makes time available for each child one-on-one.

■ *Interacting with her children.* The INFP mother spends time playing with her children side by side when they are young — making yarn dolls or clay figures, playing catch, or reading books together. As they get older, she finds other ways to engage them and interact with them.

■ *'Tuning in' to feelings.* The INFP mother pays especially close attention to her children's feelings, really listening, trying to understand, and finding appropriate ways to respond. She is also comfortable sharing her own feelings with her children, inviting them to listen and understand her feelings as well as their own.

■ *Building happy childhood memories.* The INFP mother is dedicated to creating good times for her children, making sure they experience a wide variety of fun activities traditionally associated with a happy childhood: picnics, pets, Winnie the Pooh, Girl Scouts, a day at the beach, fireflies, ice cream cones ... opportunities that will soon pass and never come again.

> 'INSIDE OUR CHILDREN, I BELIEVE, IS A TRUTH THAT TELLS THEM WHAT'S BEST FOR THEM. I AM ALWAYS LISTENING FOR THAT TRUTH.'

## STRUGGLES

■ *Focus.* "Tuned in" to feelings and responsive to everyone's viewpoint, the INFP mother may feel overwhelmed if everyone is needing something from her at the same time or when different points of view are being expressed. To whom should she listen? And whom should she "tune out?"

■ *Decision making.* The INFP mother works hard at sorting through various options to decide what's right for her children, and she tends to deal with each situation as it arises. At the time, she may feel disadvantaged by her ability to see all sides and may wonder if she is doing the right thing. Her reluctance to formulate black-and-white "rules" and policy statements for her children can leave her feeling permissive and guilty.

■ *Societal expectations.* The INFP mother struggles to balance society's expectations for order, organization, and schedules with her need (and desire) to turn to a child's need of the moment. Keeping a household running may seem at odds with the job of raising children. Her motto may be, "Pardon our mess, child development in process."

## TIPS

■ Rather than constantly doing, the INFP mother may function at her best when she has large blocks of unstructured time — time to deal with the unexpected, time to pursue creative projects, and time to think things through. Always giving to others, she can benefit from giving to herself as well —time to take an afternoon nap, read, walk, bike, or watch a movie or play.

■ Naturally tuned in to what others think and feel, the INFP mother needs to practice tuning in to her own wisdom (and trusting it!) when making decisions on behalf of her children. Because the INFP often represents a minority point of view, she may have learned to discount her own intuition about her child when facing a teacher, physician, or administrator. The INFP mother can empower herself as a parent by confidently acting on her tuned-in understanding of her child, even when others don't see it her way ... and by giving herself room to make mistakes and learn from them.

# ENFJ

## *The "Heart-to-Heart" Mother*

Expressive and warm, the ENFJ mother is adept at talking about personal concerns, both her children's and her own. She is likely to initiate heart-to-heart talks frequently and provide her children with an open forum for articulating their feelings and perspectives.

Tuned in to each child as a unique person, the ENFJ mother nurtures her children through affirmation, praise, and encouragement. She takes great pleasure when they reciprocate, offering admiration and encouragement of her, a sibling, or a friend.

Organized and energetic, the ENFJ mother is a competent, efficient family manager. She is involved in her children's lives, providing structure, direction, and guidance.

The ENFJ mother is also socially adept, relating well to people wherever she goes. She strives to keep her children connected to family, neighborhood, and the larger community.

### STRENGTHS

■ *Communication skills.* The ENFJ mother provides understanding, closeness, and emotional support through open communication. She has a keen interest in her children's feelings and wants them to feel free to express themselves. She may also express her own feelings clearly and work at being understood by her children.

■ *Organization.* The ENFJ mother keeps day-to-day living and special projects organized and moving along. Methodical and energetic, she gets a lot done and may seem like "supermom" to other mothers.

■ *Resourcefulness.* Enthusiastic and imaginative, the ENFJ mother brings a creative flair to everything she does. Her children are sure to delight in her theme birthday parties, dress-up ideas, and involvement in the class play. She in turn takes pleasure in their creativity, imagination, and fantasy play.

■ *People orientation.* The ENFJ mother places a high value on her own relationships and her children's relationships with friends, family, and community.

> 'WE HAVE SO MANY GOOD TALKS, I THINK I UNDERSTAND MY CHILDREN BETTER THAN THEY UNDERSTAND THEMSELVES.'

She encourages her children to extend themselves through service as well as friendship. She may, for example, organize a neighborhood play group to help a shy child make friends.

### STRUGGLES

■ *People or order?* Committed to cultivating close relationships and getting things done, the ENFJ mother may feel guilty or conflicted when she must choose one or the other. She finds it stressful to focus on her children and have fun knowing there are schedules and deadlines to meet ... and much to be accomplished before the day is over.

■ *Backing off.* Intense and personally involved with each child, the ENFJ mother may worry about being "overbearing" and "bossy." She tries to listen without jumping to conclusions and be less directive with a child's decision-making.

■ *Objectivity.* Sensitive to her children's anger, pain, bickering, and compliments, the ENFJ mother struggles to handle family situations objectively and avoid responding to children's attempted manipulations. Emotionally expressive, she may "fly off the handle," or she may attempt to use affection to diffuse or control difficult situations.

### TIPS

■ Humor is a wonderful way to diffuse the down side of the ENFJ's natural intensity. Insightful about human nature, she is quick to laugh at herself and the situation if someone helps her see it from a comic perspective. Harmony can be quickly restored when irritations are turned into mutual family jokes.

■ Although she is people-oriented, the ENFJ mother is drained by the chaos, noise, confusion, and multiple demands of children on a day-to-day basis. She needs some peace and quiet each day. A walk or lunch by herself can help her re-energize. She can also benefit from opportunities to engage in lively, heart-to-heart discussions with a close friend or group of friends beyond her immediate family.

# I N T J

## *The "Individual Integrity" Mother*

Individualistic and independent, the INTJ mother is both a role model and teacher of how to be an individual and live life with integrity. She is introspective, defining her own success from within, and generally confident in her decisions. She is unlikely to be persuaded by her children saying, "But all the other mothers are doing it."

The INTJ is competent in providing for her children's basic needs, but she is likely more focused on developing their self-esteem and confidence. Observant and insightful, she puts great importance on independent thinking and self-sufficiency, yet she is comfortable providing protection and boundaries.

Self-motivated and intense, the INTJ works hard and takes life seriously. As a mother, she lives for those moments when she can impart knowledge and offer her children perspectives on life and important issues.

> 'MY KIDS ARE BETTER OFF ARGUING THEIR OWN POINT OF VIEW THAN TELLING ME, "BUT EVERYONE ELSE IS DOING IT."'

## STRENGTHS

■ *Non-conformity.* The INTJ mother follows the beat of her own drum and is able to support a child who is different from the crowd. She respects each one's individuality, encouraging him or her to "think for yourself" and "act on your own beliefs." Because of her non-conformity and inner drive, she may break stereotypes and provide her children with a role model of what a non-traditional woman can be.

■ *Thoughtfulness.* A natural teacher, the INTJ mother is intellectually concerned with addressing the complexities inherent in a child's everyday life. She accepts very few situations at face value, lifting the day-to-day to a higher level of importance and meaning. In discussing the broad lessons of life, she is respectful of a child's questions and reasoning.

■ *Expecting those around her to do their best.* The INTJ mother lives with high standards, encouraging self-motivation and improvement ... from herself and others. She expects her children to stretch themselves, accept the challenges of life, and do their best despite obstacles along the way.

■ *Commitment.* Because she takes life seriously, the INTJ mother often chooses an issue, job, or project to which she fully and tirelessly commits herself. Her children may catch the spirit and learn the meaning of persistance as they watch her persevere.

## STRUGGLES

■ *Noise and confusion of family life.* The INTJ mother is drained by much of the hubbub of raising children: intrusions, noise, bickering, chatter, messes, and disorder. She may find it difficult to relate to several children at once, preferring instead some one-on-one time with each child.

■ *Mothering confidence.* Despite her commitment to doing the job of mothering right, the INTJ mother may struggle with not feeling like a "natural" mother. Believing she is different from other mothers, she may feel inadequate if she compares herself to more domestic mothers who have a house full of homey nick-nacks and daughters with bows and braids.

■ *Leading a balanced life.* The INTJ mother finds it difficult to find the right balance between her "accomplishment self" and "mother self." Wanting to tackle any responsibility with 100% effort, she may wonder where to put her focus and energy — sometimes she ignores her own competency needs for the sake of the family and sometimes she feels alienated from her children because she's so involved in a project.

## TIPS

■ It is essential for the INTJ mother to have some work or project to call her own. Volunteer responsibilities and paid employment (full- or part-time) can meet her need for mental stimulation, adult conversation, time to concentrate, and a worthy goal to achieve.

■ The INTJ mother may need more time alone away from her children than many other mothers. To be her best self, the INTJ must nurture her introspection and analysis — both of which require time and space. Being physically and emotionally available to her children needs to be balanced with time for her to think, read, or listen to the silence. A walk alone, a visit to the library, or a self-improvement class are ways to renew her energy for mothering.

# ENTP

## *The "Independence" Mother*

Full of energy and confident in her own self-sufficiency and competence, the ENTP mother encourages her children — as a role model and as a teacher — to be independent and confident on their own in the world.

A "big picture" person, she points out options and possibilities along the way. Objective and logical as well, the ENTP wants her children to evaluate their choices and learn from the consequences of their own decisions.

The ENTP mother is resourceful and action-oriented. She likes going places and doing things with her children, exploring all that life has to offer. She is less concerned with rules, routines, and schedules. Introducing her children to new concepts and activities, challenging them, and stimulating their intellectual development are top priorities.

### STRENGTHS

■ *Energetic spontaneity.* The ENTP mother is "always" ready to drop what she's doing for an outing or new experience, from accepting a last-minute invitation to a museum to assisting young entrepreneurs with the start-up of a lawn care business. Seldom bogged down with day-to-day "drudgery," she can bring a breath of fresh air and a new perspective to any situation.

■ *Encouraging independence.* The ENTP mother gives her children the space they need to develop self-sufficiency and confidence. Early on, she creates and supports opportunities for them to be out on their own, mastering their independence.

■ *Teaching.* From grocery shopping to standing in line at the post office, the ENTP mother brings her children along to experience the world. A wonderful teacher of "life," she sees every activity and moment in the day as an opportunity for children to learn about life and expand their minds.

> 'WHEN I HELD MY BABIES, I ALWAYS FACED THEM OUTWARD SO THEY COULD TAKE IN THE WORLD.'

■ *Tolerance and acceptance.* The ENTP mother takes pleasure in the variety each child brings to the family. She lets children do their own thing and refrains from pigeon-holing them. In action and words, she demonstrates respect for self and others.

### STRUGGLES

■ *Inactivity.* With her need for action, variety, and independence, the ENTP mother finds it draining to be homebound with a newborn or sick child. She may also find it difficult to adjust to children who are slower paced than she.

■ *Clingy children.* If she has a child who is physically clingy or emotionally needy, the ENTP mother may worry that he or she will never be independent or self-sufficient. She also finds she's uncomfortable in the "tender loving care" role.

■ *Household routines.* Impatient with the details and schedules of day-to-day living, the ENTP mother may struggle to carry out daily routines. She may let mundane chores turn into mini-crises ... and end up doing laundry at 2 a.m. when there's no clean underwear.

### TIPS

■ The ENTP mother needs to provide herself with intellectual stimulation, variety, and situations that allow her to function independently. Whether paid or volunteer positions, part-time work may be ideal if she can be her own boss and follow a flexible schedule. She is also likely to be energized by time spent with interesting friends or engaging in solitary, physically active pursuits such as jogging.

■ The greatest gift an ENTP mother can give herself may be help in those areas where she is least comfortable. A child care provider who enjoys spending time with children at home, a reliable housekeeper, or a spouse who is a homebody may provide balance for children who thrive with tradition and routine.

# INTP

## *The "Love of Learning" Mother*

Intellectually curious and patient, the INTP mother relishes those times with a child when they are learning something interesting together. Whether they're at the zoo or computer terminal, she sparks to answering his or her "whys" with in-depth responses or new knowledge.

The INTP mother is also objective and introspective. She listens to and discusses children's ideas and questions as she would those of a peer, fostering self-esteem and confidence. Open and non-directive, she allows children the freedom to do for themselves and quietly encourages them to believe they can do it.

Independence, autonomy, intellectual development, and self-reliance are probably the INTP's highest priorities for her children. An avid reader, she naturally imparts an appreciation and love of reading as well.

Drawn to all types of learning, the INTP may also value her mothering experience for all the new insights about life it provides her.

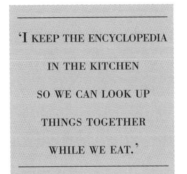

'I KEEP THE ENCYCLOPEDIA

IN THE KITCHEN

SO WE CAN LOOK UP

THINGS TOGETHER

WHILE WE EAT.'

### STRENGTHS

■ *Fostering her child's intellectual development.* The INTP mother has respect for her child's mind, thinking, and reasoning ... regardless of his or her age. Her goal is to shape her children's intellectual development, taking seriously their thoughts, ideas, and questions. She enjoys watching how they absorb and use new information.

■ *Teaching.* Desiring to meet her children's need to learn and know, the INTP mother is born to teach. She instills a love of learning by finding ways to build on a child's natural curiosity. Beyond tirelessly answering a multitude of questions, she enjoys leading him or her to new books, real-life experiences, or hands-on activities.

■ *Encouraging independence.* The INTP mother gives her children the space they need to develop independence. Although it might be easier for her to carry out a particular task herself, she can back off and let them try to do things for themselves so they

will begin to master the task. She lets her children test themselves and has high aspirations for their competency ... but she seldom pushes.

■ *Calmness.* The INTP mother is usually tolerant and calm, not highly critical of children's mistakes — she may see them as learning experiences! She seldom gets upset if they do something that displeases her. Her children may find her a model of patience, kindness, and fairness.

### STRUGGLES

■ *Noise and confusion of family life.* The INTP is exhausted by children's non-stop chatter, constant activity, lack of self-control, and their never-ending demands for her to look, listen, and respond. She may retreat, physically and emotionally.

■ *Routines.* The INTP mother is likely to struggle every time a family member needs to meet a schedule. Getting young children dressed, fed, and out the door for school on time or keeping them on task for bathing, teeth brushing, and bed times can seem like overwhelming tasks.

■ *Singular focus.* When she is focused on reading, thinking, or work, the INTP's children may feel as though they can't break through her concentration. She may worry that she seems distant and detached.

### TIPS

■ The INTP mother can benefit from setting aside regular times when she can turn inward and lose herself in reading, thought, or work. Energized by time alone to think, her "mind time" is a necessity, not a luxury. To do her best mothering, the INTP may need to get up early, stay up late, or use children's nap time to read, daydream, or gaze out the window in thought.

■ Believing she is different from other mothers, the INTP may feel uncomfortable if she compares herself to more traditional mothers. If she can learn to trust in her own unique strengths and enjoy her relationship with her children (rather than compare hers to other mothers'), she can boost her mothering confidence and take greater pleasure in day-to-day living.

# E N T J

## *The "Executive" Mother*

Competent and confident in a management role, the ENTJ mother organizes the needs and schedules of family members into a workable family system. Within the system, she provides her children with care-taking, direction, and limits, but she also gives them space to develop their own self-sufficiency and judgment.

Analytical and adept at problem-solving, the ENTJ mother listens to her children's concerns empathetically and then strategizes with them how to improve the situation — either by intervening on their behalf or backing off to let them solve problems on their own. She particularly enjoys watching them take responsibility and accomplish something they find important on their own.

Intense and insightful, the ENTJ mother is cued in to her children's intellectual and emotional development. She uses her quickness and communication skills to talk things through and help her children connect with people and better understand life.

> 'MY MIND IS ALWAYS GOING. HOW CAN I FINE-TUNE THE SYSTEM TO EVERYONE'S ADVANTAGE?'

### STRENGTHS

■ *Commitment to a family system.* Energetic and hard working, the ENTJ mother organizes a family system designed to bring out the best in each family member. Her children feel secure that someone competent is in charge, things are in order, and their needs are being addressed fairly.

■ *Fostering independence.* The ENTJ mother is focused on building her children's competence and self-sufficiency by allowing choices and autonomy within a structured family environment. She is constantly seeking the optimum balance between being directive and increasingly giving a child the freedom to make his or her own decisions.

■ *Problem-solving.* The ENTJ mother is a natural strategist and teacher. She helps children of any age think through solutions to a variety of situations, pointing out options, offering her analysis and perceptions, and instilling a "can do" attitude. When appropriate, she advocates for children at school or in any system where their best interests are not being addressed.

■ *In-depth conversations.* The ENTJ mother stimulates her children's intellectual development by engaging them in thought-provoking conversations. Interested in what they're thinking, she listens with respect, perception, and empathy. She uses ordinary life events to explain connections and broad meanings as well as to challenge children to think logically and analytically.

### STRUGGLES

■ *Busyness.* Fast paced and tightly scheduled, the ENTJ mother finds it difficult to slow down to a "normal" pace and be flexible to changes in plans. More often than she'd like, she finds herself rushing and telling her children to "hurry up." Frequently over scheduled and over committed, she may worry she's not as available to her children as she'd like to be on a regular basis.

■ *Self-criticism.* Intensely committed and wanting to be equally competent at work and family, the ENTJ mother struggles to live up to her "superhuman" expectations for herself. She may find herself constantly assessing her performance, confident about what she did well but even more self-critical when she thinks she should have done more.

■ *Letting feelings 'be.'* The ENTJ struggles to be patient with children's feelings. She is more comfortable trying to solve the problem and getting on with things than letting children experience unpleasant feelings for a while.

### TIPS

■ The ENTJ could benefit from some unstructured time for herself and her family. She needs to factor "unrushed time" into the family system. Scheduling a slow morning after a major push on a project or building in an hour of downtime mid-day can help her recharge with the time she needs to regroup and relax.

■ The ENTJ mother needs to examine realistically — and ultimately reject for herself — the myth of the "supermom." If she can accept her human vulnerabilities and limitations, she will not only enjoy life and her children more fully, she will also avoid passing on her legacy of "perfection" to the next generation.

# PART FIVE

# WHAT ABOUT DADS?

Type and fathers is an important topic! While M.O.M.S. has focused on the mothering experience, mothers and fathers alike want to know how moms and dads relate. Research indicates that at least 80% of the M.O.M.S. content applies to dads.

In recent years, we've asked fathers to respond to M.O.M.S. material. In reading the mothering profile and preference descriptions for their own type, most said they related to the strengths and uniquenesses. Some even said, "This fits me to a 'T.'"

When fathers noted differences, they did so most often in the descriptions of struggles mothers encounter. A variety of cultural, gender, and role expectations may explain the difference in struggles.

Mothers and fathers who are actively parenting today grew up with a societal and perhaps family model of mother as primary caregiver and father as head of household. This traditional mother role can be described by Sensing-Feeling-Judging characteristics, while the traditional father role calls for Sensing-Thinking-Judging attributes.

In trying to live up to their ideal, therefore, Thinking mothers have different struggles than Thinking fathers. Thinking mothers talk about lack of mothering confidence and work/family conflicts, whereas Thinking fathers say they can't relate to these concerns.

Similarly, Feeling fathers have different struggles than Feeling mothers. Feeling dads are not as likely as Feeling moms to struggle with issues of over-protecting, over-giving, or over-sacrificing.

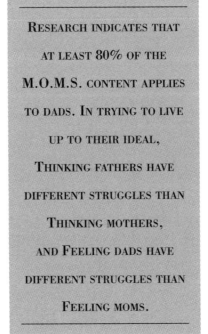

RESEARCH INDICATES THAT AT LEAST 80% OF THE M.O.M.S. CONTENT APPLIES TO DADS. IN TRYING TO LIVE UP TO THEIR IDEAL, THINKING FATHERS HAVE DIFFERENT STRUGGLES THAN THINKING MOTHERS, AND FEELING DADS HAVE DIFFERENT STRUGGLES THAN FEELING MOMS.

In addition, most Thinking women and Feeling men have had to develop their opposite preferences to fit in with cultural expectations of gender — women are Feelers and men Thinkers. As a result, Thinking moms are often better able to be emotionally supportive of children than Thinking dads. Feeling fathers are frequently more able to provide objectivity and firmness than Feeling mothers.

Mothers and fathers typically divide responsibilites within a family. Despite recent trends, mothers are usually still expected to assume primary responsibility for family and home, whether they work outside the home or not. Their struggles are typically the result of trying to meet these responsibilities.

Fathers, on the other hand, are still generally expected to be the primary wage earners. Their struggles are focused on meeting that responsibility. Stay-at-home and single-parent dads with primary responsibility for children and home related most closely to the complete mothering profile for their type.

Another area of difference between mothers and fathers is comparisons. Mothers tend to compare themselves to other mothers, neighbors, co-workers, and social peers. Trying to match every other mother's strengths, they often feel deficient and vulnerable.

Fathers tend to compare themselves to their own fathers. Given family trends over the last generation, they frequently consider themselves to be more personal and involved with their children, enhancing their sense of doing a good job.

# *What Dads Say*

| EXTRAVERSION | INTROVERSION |
|---|---|
| ■ "I'm happiest with kids who talk openly. Sitting with silence is difficult."<br><br>■ "I love active, energetic games with the kids — wrestling, chasing, tickling, getting everyone riled up."<br><br>■ "I should listen, but that's hard. I tend to talk first."<br><br>■ "I always seem to be over-extended, unable to unhook myself from work, friends, and other commitments that take energy from family." | ■ "My greatest pleasure is just watching my children."<br><br>■ "When their mother is around, I usually hang back and let her interact with the kids. When she's away, it's easier to develop my own relationship."<br><br>■ "All I do is work and family. I have no time or energy for friends or outside interests."<br><br>■ "I keep a lot inside. I wish I could interact more." |

| SENSING | INTUITION |
|---|---|
| ■ "I enjoy taking care of my kids — baths, washing hair, rocking them before bed."<br><br>■ "I'm not the primary caregiver. I'm more involved in ball games or agreeing to buy a special toy."<br><br>■ "For me, quality time is doing something together, like bowling, or apple-picking. I also like to give them some unexpected money once in a while."<br><br>■ "I tend to see things as good or bad. It's hard to accept differences or shades of gray." | ■ "I love discovering what's going on in their little minds and being there when they 'get it.'"<br><br>■ "I think I do a good job helping them see their life issues within a larger context."<br><br>■ "My favorite times are road trips when we can spend hours making up stories and talking about our ideas and dreams."<br><br>■ "It's sometimes hard for me to have realistic expectations for their age. I have to remind myself that they are little children, not adults." |

| THINKING | FEELING |
|---|---|
| ■ "My favorite times are when they fight back, argue their point of view, and let me know there is a real thinking person inside."<br><br>■ "The best part of being a father is watching my children become independent, strive toward goals, and do well academically."<br><br>■ "I like to teach. Every outing is an opportunity".<br><br>■ "Sometimes hard decisions have to be made, like discipline. I hate it when that's not interpreted as caring — because it is." | ■ "I try to be open with my feelings, hoping they'll be open in return."<br><br>■ "We have an intimate relationship. My daughter can talk to me, just like she does with her mom."<br><br>■ "While a lot of fathers would *like* to devote more time to their kids — I *do*."<br><br>■ "It's hard being the disciplinarian. Either I'm too permissive trying to be a buddy. Or I go over-board, and I'm volatile and overly punitive. I feel like a whimp or an ogre." |

| JUDGING | PERCEIVING |
|---|---|
| ■ "I'm the anchor: strong, steady, and always there. When my kids find themselves in a tough situation, they've always got me."<br><br>■ "My wife sets the house rules Monday through Friday. I try to honor her authority when I'm home on the weekends, but I have other ideas on how to raise the children."<br><br>■ "It's hard to switch gears from work to family at the end of the day. I do best if I give myself extra time to make the transition from 'work me' to 'family me.'"<br><br>■ "I'm still learning to accept the limits of my control. It's not like work. I can't make a child do what he doesn't want to do, especially an older child." | ■ "I won't feel guilty that I didn't spend enough time with my kids. I might regret not spending enough on the hard stuff — like succeeding in school."<br><br>■ "I'm good at getting kids to try new and different things, whether it's jumping off the diving board or trying an exotic food."<br><br>■ "I don't have many rules. But when the kids don't respect the few I do have — like 'be honest' — it bugs me. And I'm not sure how firm to be."<br><br>■ "Sometimes I think I'm too flexible. If I'm not careful, I find myself renegotiating curfew every night." |

# *When Mothers and Fathers Interact*

Ideally, children have both a mother and father who are active parents and can co-parent effectively, regardless of whether they are married or live in the same house. Some children are blessed to have grandparents, stepparents, siblings, aunts, or uncles who serve as co-parent.

What does type have to say about co-parenting? When parents have different preferences, children experience a home environment that is rich with a variety of personality styles. Children are free to explore who they are and can benefit from the validation that comes from knowing at least one parent shares a particular preference.

For the mother and father, differences in personality type can provide perspective and balance in co-parenting.

But differences can also cause misunderstandings, friction, and lack of consensus.

When parents share preferences, it can create a home environment that is well defined. Depending on their own preferences, children may feel in sync with the family culture, or they may feel like misfits. Similarities among parents can create a harmonious, capable parenting style. But they can also reinforce weaknesses and a sense of being stuck when facing shared struggles.

The point is to know who you are and who your co-parent is. Then you're in a position to make the most of differences, be aware of common blindspots, try to fill in as best you can for the other, and work together as a team ... so you can be effective with your children.

## EXTRAVERSION-INTROVERSION DIFFERENCES

ENERGY
INITIATIVE
FOCUS
CONNECTION

Sarah, ENTP, and Jim, INTJ, are the parents of four. Sarah says, "As two NTs, we share a vision of raising the children, but we express it differently.

"For example, we both want our kids exposed to cultural events. As the Extravert I'm the one who initiates the plans and takes them to the events. Jim doesn't always participate. I'm more engaged and actively involved with the children. But Jim will bring home an unexpected gift that's just right, and I know we've been in his thoughts.

"Knowing type has helped me understand Jim's Introversion and not interpret it as rejection or not caring. I know we are present and important in his inner world, even though he may not show his caring like I would."

Mike, ESFP, says, "Sue, ISFJ, is more of a home-body. She may share more intimate moments with our two boys, but I get them out and about.

"In addition to my job as a salesman, I coach both softball teams and have season tickets to basketball games at the local university. I also initiate father-son camping weekends with my friends. Sue's happy when we go — she gets the house to herself."

## EXTRAVERSION-INTROVERSION SIMILARITIES

Meg, ENTJ, struggled over Extraversion-Introversion differences with her first husband, an INTP, and the father of her two daughters. "Curt was good at understanding our kids' needs for privacy and silence. But I felt there weren't enough people in our lives. Curt found all-family outings, birthdays, and holidays overstimulating."

Now Meg is married to John, an ENFP. "We are both busy and on the go. We both understand everyone's need for friendships, and we want all four of our kids to enjoy an active social life. We're willing to ask the family to sacrifice on behalf of friends.

"Sometimes all the busyness gets out of hand. It's hard to say no to friends, work, volunteer commitments, and other external demands. Usually one of us starts to feel resentful because we haven't had enough time together as a couple or as a family."

Julie, INFJ, and Scott, INFP, have two teenagers. Julie says, "As Introverts, we provide a quiet, calm haven where any of us can retreat after a busy day at school or on the job. We give each person plenty of space to do his or her own thing. But it's easy to begin to feel out of touch with each other. When we do, we purposefully schedule a family outing just to do something all together."

## SENSING-INTUITION DIFFERENCES

EXPECTATIONS
CONTEXT
ANTICIPATION
SPECIFICS

Christine, ISFJ, co-parents with Peter, INTJ. "When there's a problem at school," says Christine, "I tell Peter everything that's happened and provide facts about the people involved. He takes all my specifics and comes up with a strategy for presenting our concerns.

"As a big picture person, Peter keeps me from being overly focused on details. But I'm more realistic, and we need that realism to temper Peter's expectations of the children. He's not always clear about what's appropriate behavior for a child of a particular age."

Bess, ENFJ, says, "As an Intuitive, I'm better at anticipating needs and planning ahead. Harry, ISFJ, is quick to point out what's likely to be too much. Before learning type, I resented his negativity. But now I seek his perspective as a way of making my expectations more workable."

## SENSING-INTUITION SIMILARITIES

"As a family, we've enjoyed so many rich experiences, from fishing trips and football games to holiday celebrations with our extended family," says Bill, ISTJ. "But when we face a complex problem, it's hard to see a way out."

"Our son was struggling academically in high school," explains Leslie, ESFJ. "Both of us had been good students. So we couldn't imagine what was wrong or come up with ideas for fixing it. We felt stuck until we consulted with the school counselor."

"As Intuitives, Meg, ENTJ, and I both take the long view, looking for overall trends in our children's personalities and needs," says John, ENFP. "We try to react to the situation at hand within that larger context. Neither of us wants to win the battle but lose the war."

"Still, some household details don't get our attention until there's a crisis — like no food in the refrigerator and company's coming," laughs Meg. "More than once we've argued as we push ourselves to get everything done, including mowing the lawn, planting flowers, and buying a grill for a barbecue."

## THINKING-FEELING DIFFERENCES

DIRECTNESS
COMPASSION
EMOTIONALITY
INDEPENDENCE

Raquel, ENFP, compares herself to Lou, ISTJ: "I'm emotional and can overreact. He's rational, cool, self-controlled and even-tempered. Lou teaches our daughter money management and computers. I teach her how to handle sticky people problems."

"When I'm worried about our sons," explains Mary, ENFJ, "Charles, INTP, comforts me with a rational perspective.

"We have a different approach with teachers. He's direct, and I'll do anything to avoid confrontation. If something at school is unfair, Charles is quick to call and set the situation right. We all feel protected with him."

Still, Feeling mothers say they need to smooth over what Thinking fathers say and do.

"Although he doesn't mean it," says Mary, "Charles' bluntness feels like an attack. I try to smooth things over for the boys with softer words."

"In our house," says Meg, ENTJ, "John, ENFP, takes the compassion approach, and I take the justice approach. I tell him he's gone too far giving children the benefit of the doubt. He lets me know I need to back off when I'm expecting too much. We're a good sounding board for each other.

"Sometimes I think he invites dependency. He jumps in to drive our daughter to school when she's late. I'd rather encourage self-sufficiency by letting her face the logical consequences — embarrassment with teachers and a detention."

## THINKING-FEELING SIMILARITIES

Bess, ENFJ, says, "Harry, ISFJ, and I share 50/50 in everything. If someone cooks dinner, the other cleans up. We're equally nurturing and affectionate. We both make the kids' special events a top priority, even if it means sacrificing work.

"If I go out of town, I don't make casseroles or leave notes about afterschool activities. Harry can care for the children as well as I can."

Jack, ENFJ, agrees: "I don't see a big difference between the role of the mother and that of the father. Sure, Debbie, ENFP, did the breastfeeding. But I've painted my daughter's finger nails and taken my son clothes shopping for his first dance.

"I believe a natural division of labor evolves between mother and father based on tradition, individual interests and circumstances — not gender."

Mike, ESFP, however, sees a difference. "Sue, ISFJ, is the primary caretaker and homemaker. I do the fun stuff and play the 'heavy' when the kids need to be disciplined."

"As two Thinkers, Max, ISTP, and I have a lot in common," says Kate, ENTJ. "Neither is ashamed of being strict, putting limits on kids or encouraging self-sufficiency.

"But there are differences. Max is more direct and less inclined to consider the impact of his words. He might offend a coach with an off-handed remark. I'm more likely to tone down my critical comments or keep them to myself."

## JUDGING-PERCEIVING DIFFERENCES

RULES
ROUTINES
FUN
FLEXIBILITY

"Lou, ISTJ, wants things done, and he wants them done a certain way," says Raquel, ENFP. "I prefer to start projects and keep them open, following my inspirations. To compromise, we've come to this motto: 'Done is better than perfect.'"

Kate, ENTJ, says, "Max, ISTP, does fun really well, whether it's bike rides, ball games, or outings. He takes care of all the gear needed and has fun interacting with the kids. While they're playing, I'm free to get a lot done.

"We've all come to accept the fact that Max starts a lot of projects and doesn't finish them according to our timetable. At first the kids felt let down. Now they factor his style into their requests. In fact, I'm beginning to admire his way of doing things for as long as he feels like it, and no more."

*Illustration from Parenting Style Slide Set*

*Family schedules and routines can cause friction between Judging - Perceiving parents. While a Judging parent believes bedtime is bedtime, a Perceiving parent may lose track of time enjoying the moment.*

## JUDGING-PERCEIVING SIMILARITIES

"With two Js for parents, our kids know how things work in our house — the rules, consequences, routines," says Bess, ENFJ. "Harry, ISFJ, and I like order, and we're consistent in setting limits and providing structure. Our way of doing bedtimes, getting ready for school, or celebrating birthdays and holidays is almost ritualized. We're especially sensitive to the stress transitions cause and work hard to keep the children in a familiar routine even when we travel."

"On the downside," adds Christine, ISFJ, "neither Peter, INTJ, nor I is good at making spontaneous fun. Sometimes I realize the weekend is over and we've taken care of all our chores, but we haven't had one ounce of fun together as a family."

"A household run by two Ps is different," says Mike, ENFP. "Sue, INFP, the kids, and I have lots of freedom. People have said our spontaneous lifestyle seems out of control and stressful, but we love it.

"On the other hand, sometimes we lose track of time and forget things like soccer practice or getting the recycling out in time for pick-up."

# PART SIX

# MAKING PRACTICAL

# USE OF TYPE

## Children and Parenting

After learning about their own type preferences, many parents want to use basic type concepts to better understand their children and improve their parenting effectiveness. M.O.M.S. offers some suggestions, but you will also want to consider the materials on children and parenting listed in "Recommended Further Resources" on pages 59 to 61.

### Guessing Your Child's Type

A common question parents ask is "How early can my child be 'typed?'" M.O.M.S. finds that many eight- to 10-year-olds are able to grasp the concepts of personality type, identify most of their own preferences, and even guess their parents' types. For younger children, we believe parents can make useful guesses about preferences, remembering that they're hypotheses only and that some preferences evidence themselves before others. That's OK.

Some type experts believe signs of Extraversion-Introversion and Judging-Perceiving emerge first and are easier to guess in young children than Sensing-Intuition and Thinking-Feeling. Still, some parents say they knew early on that their child had a preference for Thinking or Feeling, for example. As more research on type and children is completed, we will know more about the development of preferences and how they are expressed in the early years.

Before children can express themselves well verbally, your hypotheses will be based on your observations of their behavior and your understanding of type theory. Keep in mind, however, that behaviors can spring from different motivations. For example, a preschooler may refuse to participate in one of the teacher's innovative group activities. Is that because he's a Thinker and doesn't see the point? Or an Introvert who needs to observe others before trying it himself? Or something else?

Type is great for understanding behavior but less effective predicting it. As children mature, they can help you understand their differences by telling you how they see things and the thoughts behind their actions. Take time to listen. As you try to guess your child's type, you will also want to keep your hypotheses open and resist labeling. Children are developing, and regardless of their type, they need all kinds of opportunities and experiences. Be open to new information and be willing to change your hypothesis as you learn more about your child. Labeling a child, whether it's accurate or not, may limit who he or she can be.

> AS YOU TRY TO GUESS YOUR CHILD'S TYPE, YOU WILL ALSO WANT TO KEEP YOUR HYPOTHESES OPEN AND RESIST LABELING.

And don't be lulled into thinking that type explains everything about a child and provides a fool-proof recipe for how to raise him or her. Each child is much more than type. Birth order, family configuration, gender, physical differences, ethnic and family culture, socioeconomic influences, intelligence, and other aptitudes all combine to create great variations among children of the same type.

## What Are Your Child's Preferences?

### EXTRAVERSION-INTROVERSION

Does your child burst in the door after school full of news? Or does she enter quietly, respond to questions with a simple yes or no and head for her room?

Many Extaverted children say that until they've told someone about the events of the day, those events haven't really happened. One mother described her Extraverted child as a chatterbox with never an unspoken thought.

Introverted children say they need to be alone for a while after school to recharge. After being with peers, teachers, and other caregivers all day, they don't want another conversation with mom. They might not feel like talking again until dinner or bedtime.

Extraverted children prefer to be with others rather than be alone. They may enjoy group projects and doing homework with friends. A special birthday party might involve hosting the whole class for games, music, balloons, and clowns.

Introverted children are apt to spend their time playing alone or reading by themselves, even at an early age. Their idea of a special birthday party might be to invite just one friend for pizza, a movie, and a sleep-over.

One mother says, "When we pulled into our driveway after a two-week family vacation, my Extraverted son immediately ran down the street to see what was happening with his buddies. He was bored relating to the same four people. My Introverted son went to his room and shut the door. Doing everything as a foursome for two weeks had deprived him of the privacy he needs."

### SENSING-INTUITION

Sensing children are hands-on learners. Until they've had direct experience, it isn't quite real. They tend to be literal, needing accuracy and trusting the facts. If dad suggests his Sensing daughter was 10 minutes late for dinner, she'll likely respond that she was only nine minutes late.

A Sensing fifth grader complained about a school assignment — he was to make up a fictional country, draw a map, and then answer questions based on his map. "To me this is a complete waste of time. It isn't

real. How will they know if the answers are right or wrong? I'd rather work with a real country and real map."

Sensing children may prefer reading nonfiction, biographies, encyclopedias, game manuals, news–papers, and magazines over fiction. If a friend suggests turning a bus seat into a magic carpet, the Sensing child may respond, "There's no such thing."

Still, Sensing children often take pleasure in little things — details on a miniature doll, putting on a favorite shirt still warm from the dryer, or the smell of a new spring morning.

Without as much concern for what's real, Intuitive children enjoy coming up with new ideas and imagining. They may relish making up a story from a picture or pretending the closet is a treasure cave.

*Illustration from Parenting Style Slide Set*

*Extraverted parents like to get kids out to experience the world. But Introverted children may prefer to stay at home, playing quietly on their own.*

"My Intuitive stepdaughter decided to publish a family newspaper, *The Tiddledy Winks News*, and had great fun writing stories for the first issue," reports one mother. "She later dropped it when her interest turned to another inspiration — starting a business creating greeting cards on the computer."

Intuitive children often prefer school assignments that let them be original, such as illustrating a poem, creating a board game, or choreographing a dance. Sometimes, however, they struggle with the practicalities and end up with something that falls short of the initial vision.

Intuitive children might not be aware of their surroundings or the here-and-now, going through the day like an "absent-minded professor" and forgetting such necessities as lunch or bus money. They tend to be book learners, focusing on the big picture and abstract concepts rather than needing as much direct experience and facts as Sensing children.

## THINKING-FEELING

Thinking children ask lots of "hows" and "whys." They need to know the reasons behind questions and requests, not to mention the logic of how things work. Teachers have to earn the Thinker's respect through fair rules, impartial consequences, not playing favorites, and being knowledgeable. Motivated by achievement and competition, Thinkers tend to measure their performance by objective standards and accomplishments.

The Thinking child's interest in principles and truth can make him or her a good debater, assertively and objectively arguing a critical point. One grandmother told her Thinking grandchild he had to get his parents' permission if he wanted to stay the night. The boy responded, "Great! I love arguing with my parents."

Thinking children tend to show love through concrete actions and responsibility, rather than "mushy" talk. They may back off if others appear overly affectionate, and they may avoid or cut short discussions of feelings.

Though they do not intend to be unkind, their bluntness and often unawareness of feelings can sometimes offend or hurt.

Feeling children are people-pleasers, seeking praise, feedback, and the feeling of being special. They are motivated by relationships and the desire to be helpful and well-liked. Interested in getting along with others, they may avoid conflict. Most report an inability to work well in friction-filled situations. A friendly dinnertime debate may sound like fighting to a Feeling child and dampen his or her appetite.

For Feeling children, praising the deed is the same as praising the child. One Feeling child came home from softball practice saying the coach liked her. When asked why she thought so, she responded, "Because he said I was a good hitter."

The opposite is true as well. If Feelers believe a teacher doesn't like them, they'll be distracted from the learning at hand. Feeling children need plenty of affection, acceptance, and closeness to flourish.

## JUDGING-PERCEIVING

Judging children need structure, limits, and routine to feel secure. When they wake up in the morning, they might ask mom or dad what the plan for the day is. They like to know what to expect and when.

Flexibility is hard for a Judging child. A preschooler may have a temper tantrum if activities don't go as planned or the babysitter fixes lunch differently than mother usually does. Transitions can be especially stressful, whether it's changing activities or welcoming a new sibling. Judging children often need preparation and extra time to adapt to changes.

Doing things the "right way" is important to Judgers. So they'll want to know the rules. Adults might be impressed with their responsibility and maturity, but friends consider them bossy if they try to make everyone adhere to rules or do things the right way.

Judging children are generally on time and organized. Deadlines are stressful, so they tend to work steadily to avoid a last-minute crisis. They prefer to finish their work before feeling free to play.

Perceiving children thrive on freedom and spontaneity. They don't like waking up to hear that the day is all planned for them. They prefer to go with the flow, doing what they want when they want and being open to opportunities as they arise.

The very routine that makes a Judging child feel secure can make a Perceiving child feel tied down. "When Justin drops by at 5:30 with a great new video game, why do we have to stop for dinner if I'm not hungry?"

Gifted at living in the moment and enjoying life as it happens, Perceivers are naturals at trying new things and adapting to the unexpected. They are generally tolerant of others. Friends say they're fun-loving and laid back, but parents often worry about lack of follow-through and organization. Work and play go together, and they try to make their work fun (expect a water fight when they wash the car).

More process than product oriented, Perceiving children typically wait until the last minute to do school assignments or handle their responsibilities. Fast-approaching deadlines can produce a burst of energy, focus, and productivity.

## When Parents and Children Interact

When a child is born, he or she enters a family culture of values, mindsets, traditions, and lifestyles that have been shaped by parents and generations of grandparents and great grandparents. Societal and ethnic "norms" certainly play a role. Yet a family's culture is closely related to the parents' type preferences.

When a child's preferences match those of the family culture, parents often remark how easily he or she fits in and gets along with other family members. When a child's preferences are different from those of the parents, he or she may be regarded as "challenging." Of course, family cultures are different. The same behavior may be encouraged in one family and punished in another. For example, a child who speaks up for him or herself may be considered assertive in one family while another family might regard such behavior as disobedient.

### Battle of Wills

*When Judging parents raise Judging children, the result is often a battle of wills. Judging parents want to exert maximum control over homelife, leaving minimum, if any, space for Judging children to develop their own structure and exercise their own judgments. One Judging adult remembers, "As a child I desperately wanted to help my mother in the kitchen. But she wouldn't even let me load the dishwasher for fear I'd do it wrong. That made me feel powerless and resentful." Regardless of age, each Judger in the family needs to have his or her own domain of control, whether it's one drawer in the kitchen, the family calendar, or a play area.*

Type knowledge can make parents more aware of the unique culture they are providing ... and offer some clues for more enjoyable family living.

M.O.M.S. research indicates that, when parent and child share the same preferences, they talk about a special bond, understanding, and compatibility. But there is also the danger of stepping on each other's toes or reinforcing weaknesses. Some parents see their own shortcomings in children who are similar and try to fix or heal those problems in the children rather than in themselves.

Still, most misunderstandings, worry, and mistrust occur in families when a parent and child have different type preferences. Differences can produce feelings of superiority or inadequacy — "Either my way is right and his is wrong, or he's right and I'm wrong."

It takes more mindfulness, and therefore more energy, to raise a child who is different.

Knowledge and use of personality type can help families move beyond power struggles, win-lose dynamics, and getting kids to "shape up." It can help parents create a family environment where differences are respected and each person is allowed to be him- or herself. The issue becomes: "You're that way, I'm this way, and we love each other. How are we going to work it out?" With an understanding of type, your task is to give your children the benefit of your experience, perspective, and skills without giving them the impression that their natural way is wrong or undependable.

On the positive side, you may admire the ways your child is different from you: "Chris is so outgoing, I could never be so comfortable with people," or "Stephanie is so imaginative, I don't know where she gets it." Perhaps you will even learn from your children! But they will become their best selves when you give them a special place within the family to develop their preferences.

### EXTRAVERTED PARENT - INTROVERTED CHILD

The Extraverted parent often questions what's wrong with an Introverted child. Worried that the young Introvert doesn't have enough friends, spends too much time alone, and isn't interested in joining groups or organized activities, the Extravert wonders if the child is depressed or suffering from a physical illness. Extraverted parents can wear themselves out trying to get an Introverted child to perk up, join up, and have a social life.

The Introverted child may feel her parents are too intrusive, pushy, and always "in my face." Hounding can make her feel inadequate. One Introverted adult tells how his Extraverted mother was so worried about his lack of friends that she considered adopting a child: "She saw it as a way of providing me with the company she thought I so desperately needed but couldn't get on my own. It made me feel like a real loser."

On the plus side, many Introverted children talk about how Extraverted parents are a help speaking for them in uncomfortable situations, teaching them how to meet people, and introducing them to new kids in the neighborhood.

### INTROVERTED PARENT - EXTRAVERTED CHILD

When an Introverted parent raises an Extraverted child, it is often the parent who feels inadequate and energyless. Introverted parents say, "This child is sucking the life from me!" An active preschooler who wants constant interaction with mom can push the Introvert beyond her limits to the point of suddenly exploding, surprising them both by her quick change of demeanor. Introverted parents may criticize older Extraverted children for what they consider "unnecessary talking," whether in the car or watching a movie.

Extraverted children often describe an Introverted parent as too distant. The parent may be physically present but so lost in his or her own thoughts that the child finds it hard to break through and get his or her attention. Extraverted children also report worrying about an Introverted parent's isolation. The child may feel torn when accepting a social invitation knowing it will leave mom at home alone. Extraverted children want their parents to have friends, belong, and be with them as part of a group.

On the plus side, Extraverted adults say they appreciate the distance and privacy their Introverted parent gave during the teen years.

### SENSING PARENT - INTUITIVE CHILD

Sensing parents see an Intuitive child's dreamy, uneven ways and wonder how he will ever make it on his own.

## S-N & Intelligence

*Sensing and Intuitive types define intelligence differently. A Sensing mother may discount her Intuitive child's insights and grasp of major themes if a report is messy or full of typographical errors. Likewise, an Intuitive father may make a Sensing child feel slow if she can't follow his quick transitions of thought, needs more time to absorb facts, or remembers the details of a lesson while forgetting the main idea. As they grow, Intuitive children may be frustrated with parents who are too literal and conservative, and a Sensing child may find it's difficult to trust parents' intuitive leaps.*

They may see their role as giving an Intuitive a dose of reality — calling attention to careless mistakes and asking detailed questions about how he intends to find the time to accomplish his big idea or pay for it.

The Intuitive may misinterpret his Sensing parents' involvement as "throwing a bucket of cold water on all my ideas." While Sensing parents might diligently show their love by managing a child's physical needs, the young Intuitive may discount those efforts, not noticing what they've done or realizing how much time it takes. One Intuitive tells how she noticed a bath tub ring at college and assumed the water was different in her dorm than at home. She had been oblivious to the daily scrubbing her Sensing mother gave the tub.

On the positive side, Intuitive children say they are often overwhelmed by the practicalities of implementing an idea and value a Sensing parent's help — typing a story, sewing a Halloween costume, or purchasing ingredients for a surprise birthday cake.

## INTUITIVE PARENT - SENSING CHILD

When Intuitive parents raise a Sensing child, they may discount her need for concrete, specific information. One Intuitive mother reports having asked her Sensing son to clean his room only to discover an hour later that it looked much the same. The boy explained that he had emptied the waste basket and stopped because she hadn't told him exactly what she expected him to do. Giving specific directions instead of offering only the general concept is something Sensing children need but Intuitive parents often forget to do.

Intuitive parents resist focusing on the practicalities of day-to-day living, causing some Sensing children to feel ungrounded and wonder who or what they can count on. When a Sensing child asks what's for dinner, and the Intuitive mother says she hasn't come up with an idea, the child may feel shaky and insecure.

On the positive side, Sensing children often say they appreciate an Intuitive parent's imagination, particularly when they need help with school assignments that require originality and creativity.

## THINKING PARENT - FEELING CHILD

Thinking parents often report being perplexed by a Feeling child's sensitivity. "How can I correct poor behavior when she bursts into tears over a look sideways?"

They may also be concerned that the Feeling child appears to need "unlimited" emotional support — too many compliments, too much personal attention, or too much comfort. Thinking parents find it hard to believe that a Feeling child's emotional needs are genuine rather than manipulative. They might try to toughen her up by telling her to stop crying or keep her feelings under control.

Feeling children sometimes do not feel loved enough by a Thinking parent. Because they crave affection, praise, and appreciation, they may miss dad or mom's Thinking expressions of caring — respect and space to practice independence. One Feeling child told her Thinking mother, "I'm just someone who needs a lot of compliments!"

A Thinking mother reports, "When my Feeling son would come home from school saying he'd had a terrible day and no one liked him, I used to try to convince him it wasn't true. Now I respond with 'Poor darling, would milk and cookies make you feel better?'"

On the positive side, Feeling children often say they find comfort in the way a Thinking parent helps in a difficult situation: getting behind the emotions to look at it objectively and figure out how to apply problem-solving skills.

## FEELING PARENT - THINKING CHILD

Feeling parents often describe a Thinking child as not being cuddly or chummy enough and say they feel rejected or attacked from time to time. "I go to give her a big hug and she backs away," says a Feeling mother.

Another parent says, "Once I was praising my Thinking son, and he started to walk away. I asked, 'Don't you like to hear compliments?' He responded, 'Sure, but with you it takes too long.'" Feeling parents sometimes misinterpret their Thinking child's emotional distance and objectivity as lack of caring or love. From the Thinking child's perspective, Feeling parents can be intrusive, asking too many personal questions and initiating conversations about feelings. Young Thinkers also say Feeling parents are overly involved and protective, not giving them the room they need to challenge and practice self-reliance.

Sensitivity is another issue. Says one Thinking teenager, "I try to make a joke, tease him, or argue a point. But Dad takes it personally. I don't mean to hurt his feelings, but he's overly sensitive about everything."

On the plus side, Thinking children say that when they're mad or sad, Feeling parents seem to care. "My mother gives me the opportunity to talk about how I feel," says a Thinking teen. "By communicating my feelings, I'm better able to understand and manage them."

## JUDGING PARENT - PERCEIVING CHILD

Judging parents often find Perceiving children exasperating: "I ask her to do a job and she gets sidetracked by something more interesting." "His room looks like a cyclone hit it." "She waits until the last minute to do homework." "He could be Number One in his class if he'd only apply himself."

Judging parents worry that their Perceiving child will not find her way in the world. They may try to "make" their young Perceiver more focused, more responsible, more organized, and more considerate.

The result can be a power struggle between a parent trying to control and a child bent on resisting control and proving her way is fine.

From the child's point of view, a Judging parent's emphasis on structure, planning, and order is superfluous. The Perceiver doesn't need it to feel secure and may in fact feel confined, limited, and unaccepted.

One Perceiving adult says, "As a child, I liked having a messy room and an easygoing relationship with my things. My piles were my friends. My parents never understood, but they were kind enough to shut my bedroom door and forget about it."

On the plus side, Perceiving children say they appreciate knowing what it takes to survive in a Judging world and having been "pushed" to develop many of those skills.

### PERCEIVING PARENT - JUDGING CHILD

When Perceiving parents raise a Judging child, they often feel put upon to make structure and plans when they don't feel the need. "My son wakes up each morning asking what's the plan for the day, and I don't have one yet," says one Perceiving parent.

Perceiving parents sometimes question what's wrong with a child so focused on boundaries and control. "Sure, I bought the boombox for my daughter to play CDs in her room. But I wish she'd lighten up and be more gracious about sharing when she comes home and finds me listening to it while I fix her dinner."

A Perceiver's casual approach can leave a Judging child feeling insecure and uncared for. He often wonders, "Is anyone in charge here? Or do I have to make the order and plans...." Sometimes a Judging child will try to organize a Perceiving parent by making to-do lists to be completed while he is at school or saying an activity begins 15 minutes earlier than it does to be on time.

One Judging mother says, "When I was a child I had no bedtimes or curfews. I could do pretty much what I wanted. I doubted whether my parents really cared. If a friend called to make plans, I'd pretend to ask my parents if it was okay."

On the positive side, Judging children say they appreciate growing up knowing how to balance life. Driven to get their work done, they know there's always fun to be had and that work can sometimes wait.

## General Type/Children Tips

■ *Turn down the volume on Judging (I'm right, I'm in control). Turn up the volume on Perceiving (acceptance, understanding).*

We have as much to learn from our children as we have to teach. Although it's true that we bring experience, maturity, and skills to the parenting experience, no one knows what's best for another in every situation. Too many of us treat our children as projects to manage, control, and direct, or as problems to fix.

In many ways a child is like a seed: each one holds the innate potential to grow, flourish, and blossom in its unique way. There's no sense trying to shape a lily into a rose. Similarly, a parent's responsibility is like that of a gardener. Instead of trying to make a plant grow, the gardener tries to provide the right mix of soil, sun, water, and nutrients, then waits patiently for the flower to unfold.

■ *Do not treat all children alike.*

Some parents believe fairness means treating every child the same. If Sue gets new shoes, then so should Jim, even if his are still good. But to be truly fair, children need to be treated as individuals. An active Extraverted child may need to be in more classes and activities than her Introverted brother. Try to tune in to individual differences and needs and act/react accordingly.

■ *Recognize differences and similarities in your style and theirs.*

When parent and child experience personality differences, parents often fear something is "wrong" with the child and find it difficult to be approving and non-judgmental. The child's self-esteem may begin to suffer. Or there might be serious misunderstandings. Instead, look for the strengths of a child's style, view the differences as gifts for growth, and give him or her permission to be who he or she is meant to be. Parent and child can work toward flexing toward each other when it's important. But you both must remember to reserve space for individual preferences and style. Mutual respect and negotiation is the ideal.

When parent and child are similar, understanding and communication are usually easier. But parents must be warned about seeing their own weaknesses in their child. Be careful not to try to fix weaknesses or reinforce blind spots. Allow enough room for each child to develop his or her own preferences.

■ *Learn to speak and listen in your
   child's language.*

Individuals with the preference for Sensing respond best to communication that is factual, specific, and sequential. Intuitives prefer enthusiastic, imaginative language. Thinking types respond to brief, concise statements that point out the reasons why. Feeling types want empathy and personal interest expressed. Communication can be most effective when differences are taken into account.

■ *Be sensitive to the obstacles to good
   type development.*

Our culture and school systems overvalue Extraversion, Sensing, Thinking, and Judging and undervalue the opposites — except when it comes to girls. Thinking girls grow up somewhat out of step with cultural expectations (women = Feeling), as do boys with a preference for Feeling. In addition, families have styles and preferences for certain personality traits. A child who has a preference undervalued by other family members can begin to believe there is something wrong with him or her. Be sensitive and supportive, and empower children with preferences for Introversion, Intuition, Thinking/Feeling, and Perceiving. Encourage them to develop and trust their gifts and wisdom.

■ *Check out negative conclusions.*

Despite good intentions and type awareness, no one can know what's going on inside another person day in and day out. So when you've come to a negative conclusion about a child's behavior — "She's doing it to irritate me," or "He doesn't care" — take time to check it out. "This is how I'm interpreting your behavior. Is that correct? Or is there something else going on I should know about?" Often what parents consider misbehavior was well-intentioned and makes sense when the full story comes to light in the context of the child's personality type.

---

## Tips for Raising a Child with a Preference for...

| EXTRAVERSION | INTROVERSION |
|---|---|
| ■ Allow play and socializing after school and before bed or naptime. Extraverts need people time before starting homework and winding down time before falling asleep. | ■ Allow time alone after school, day care, or other activity. Introverts need privacy to regroup before doing homework or continuing with the next scheduled activity. |
| ■ Make a conscious effort to hear about the Extravert's day when he or she comes home from preschool, football practice, a party, or summer job. | ■ Consider making bedtime or dinner the time to check in with an Introvert, rather than right after school. He or she will be better able to talk about the day having had some time alone to process it. |
| ■ When you need to discuss something important, try talking together while doing — taking a walk or drive, planting a garden, or eating at a restaurant. | ■ Instead of starting conversations with a question, invite an Introvert to listen to your thoughts first. |
| ■ Include extended family, friends, and their families for family get-togethers. Young Extraverts enjoy social networks beyond their immediate family and the energy of other people in their homes. | ■ Realize silent companionship is relationship-building with Introverts. |
|  | ■ Try written communications. Say what's important in a note. Have your young Introvert do the same — suggest he or she write you a letter. |

## *Tips for Raising a Child with a Preference for...*

| SENSING | INTUITION |
|---|---|

- Supplement directions with details, examples, and specific how-tos. A global directive like "research your report" will not produce notecards and a bibliography.
- Teach a Sensing child through hands-on, direct experiences. Provide real-life experiences to supplement or clarify book learning at school.
- Engage the Sensing child's senses when making a point. Ask him or her to repeat what you've said — taste, smell, and feel it. Demonstrate the action, like dropping an egg on the pavement to encourage use of a bike helmet.
- Realizing a Sensing child can get stuck in "what is," play the "what if" game for new ideas: "What if you miss the bus home, what can you do?" "What if you're locked out?" Debrief experiences: "What could you have done? If it happens next time ..."

- Expect bursts of productive energy and inspired activity followed by extended periods of doing nothing and showing no interest in much of anything.
- When there's a project to be done, start with the big picture and don't offer too many details. Be able to answer questions about specifics as the project unfolds.
- Know that an Intuitive is attracted to many new ideas and possibilities, but don't expect him or her to follow through on everything, whether it's activities or friends.
- Give Intuitives the time and space they need to play with ideas and dream, no matter how unrealistic or absurd. Wait until the initial inspiration cools before helping them be more realistic.

| THINKING | FEELING |
|---|---|

- Respect a Thinker's need to know why by giving the reasons behind your requests and decisions. "Unload the dishwasher now because I want the kitchen cleaned up before cooking dinner." "I'm letting you borrow the car because I trust your judgment."
- Ask for even the young Thinker's help when problem-solving family issues, both large and small. When rules are broken, plans are changing or behavior needs correcting, ask what he or she thinks would be fair or a reasonable solution.
- Motivate with goals and objective rewards, such as points, prizes, or special privileges.
- Provide opportunities for a Thinker to practice independence and self-sufficiency.

- Realize a Feeler is motivated by the relationship. He'll play his best softball if dad is the coach. She'll write her best story if she thinks the teacher likes her.
- Appreciate and support a Feeling child's efforts to bring the family together and create happy times. Give plenty of praise, compliments, and positive feedback. Don't expect a Feeler to know he or she did well or is loved without hearing it from others.
- Meet a young Feeler's needs for dependency and closeness early on. Staying longer with a clingy preschooler may make separation easier in kindergarten.
- When you want to correct behavior, sit close, hold his or her hand, and make sure he or she feels loved before you address the problem. Do it gently.

| JUDGING | PERCEIVING |
|---|---|

- Provide household structure, even if it's just one or two routines a day, to help your Judging child feel grounded and comfortable.
- Begin the day by telling your child about any plans, even if they are sketchy or still in process. "You have a piano lesson at 4:30, and I'll be at Aunt Mae's all afternoon."
- Give a Judging child something to control to develop planning and organization skills rather than always following your plan. Do it his or her way, when appropriate.
- Reward a Judger with more responsibility and more authority.

- Allow your Perceiving children free time after school to unwind. Be careful not to over-structure their time.
- Factor playtime into any task. Perceiving children need time to explore and have fun while working. It may take twice as long as you think it should to complete a task.
- Tidy up together. Setting a big mess in order can be overwhelming to a Perceiving child. Be a model for sorting and ordering while letting your child provide most of the labor.
- Limit your expectations of follow-through. Perceivers like to start projects and sample experiences without expecting to finish them. Demand stick-to-it-ativeness in just a few key areas, and let the little stuff slide.

# *M o r e   W o r k a b l e   W o r k   C h o i c e s*

Personality type can help a mother make more workable work choices in three important ways:

■ Knowing her type can help a mother understand her potential work/family conflicts.

■ Self-knowledge can help her identify work situations that fit her best.

■ Similarly, knowing her type can make a mother more aware of work situations that would drain her in the same ways mothering does.

A mother's personality type, however, is not a good predictor of her employment status. M.O.M.S. research indicates that all three employment options — full-time employment, part-time employment, and stay-at-home full time — are represented among all 16 types of mothers.

To help you understand your personal work/family conflicts, here is what other women say about why they want to work outside the home and why they want to stay home with their children:

## *Potential Work/Family Conflicts by Personality Preference*

| | WHY I WANT TO WORK OUTSIDE THE HOME | WHY I WANT TO STAY HOME FULL TIME WITH CHILDREN |
|---|---|---|
| EXTRAVERSION | "I need to be with people. I'm too isolated at home." | "I want to focus my greatest energy on my children and family." |
| INTROVERSION | "I need blocks of solitude to concentrate, without distractions and interruptions." | "I don't have enough energy for home and work. I don't feel like I can 'do it all.'" |
| SENSING | "I need the opportunity to use my skills and be connected to the reality of the world." | "No one can take care of my children's basic needs and physically be there for them like I can." |
| INTUITION | "I need exposure to new ideas and perspectives." | "No one can develop my child's potential like I can." |
| THINKING | "I need objective validation of my competence, a sense of accomplishment and achievement." | "Parenting is my highest priority. I don't want to miss all the once-in-a-lifetime opportunities." |
| FEELING | "I need to be valued and appreciated. Also, working outside the home gives me a more objective viewpoint about my children." | "Parenting is the greatest kind of intimacy. My kids need me, and I don't want to separate from them constantly." |
| JUDGING | "I need something I can control and complete." | "I need maximum control over home life." |
| PERCEIVING | "I need the stimulation and variety work provides." | "Work involves too much juggling, structuring, and living with a schedule." |

*A Feeling-Judging mother of two preschoolers was feeling drained by her job as a bedside nurse in ways she had never experienced before. With the support of her family, she decided to try a modest job change rather than a sweeping career move. She improved her work/family balance by going to work as an office manager for doctors in private practice. Taking care of schedules, ordering supplies, and occasionally helping with patient care at work was a better balance to the emotional drains of caring for small children at home.*

Feeling women, for example, are typically drawn to the helping professions — nursing, teaching, community service. After becoming a mother, however, the Feeling woman may find herself overextended in the Feeling dimension of her jobs — caring for the needs of others at work and then coming home to care for the needs of children and family.

It is important to remember: the "mother" job is one you can't quit. You'll increase your success of balancing work and family by choosing a work situation that considers the struggles of your mothering style and doesn't drain you in the same ways.

## WHAT KIND OF WORK FITS ME BEST

| | |
|---|---|
| Extraversion | Work that lets me interact with a variety of people, away from my desk and on the go |
| Introversion | Work that gives me time for concentration and a chance to work alone |
| Sensing | Work that is practical, detailed, and requires careful observation |
| Intuition | Work that provides new perspectives and new problems to be solved |
| Thinking | Work that requires analysis and the application of logic |
| Feeling | Work that helps meet the needs of others, in a work environment where people get along |
| Judging | Work that can be managed, systematized, and structured |
| Perceiving | Work that requires adapting to and understanding changing situations rather than managing them |

Combining work-outside-the-home with family is most successful when the mother has an employment situation that fits her personality type. A mismatch between work and personality type can cause stress, fatigue, and feelings of inadequacy.

However, this is probably even more true for mothers who come home to a "second shift" of additional family and household responsibilities. Most mothers say there just isn't enough free time to adequately recharge after work.

Rather than constantly bending to fit the job, a mother needs a job that fits who she is — one that is energizing instead of draining.

YOUR HOSPITAL BENEFIT RAISED MORE MONEY THAN WE EVER RAISED BEFORE!

BENEFIT AUCTION

*Promotions, awards, and straight As let a Thinker know how well she's doing. "I used to think I could get by without taking care of myself," says a Thinker. "Then I realized raising funds for the hospital met my need to be recognized for my competence."*

# *Recommended Further Resources*

## ORGANIZATIONS

**Penley and Associates, Inc.**
604 Maple Ave. • Wilmette, IL 60091
847-251-4936 • *website:* www.momsconnection.com

*Seminars, training, materials, and consulting on parenting. If you are using this handbook in group settings, quantity discounts are available. See page 61 for information.*

**Association for Psychological Type (APT)**
9140 Ward Parkway • Kansas City, MO 64114
816-444-3500 • *website:* www.APTCentral.org

*Membership organization of type users, training, conferences, journals*

**The Center for Applications
of Psychological Type (CAPT)**
2815 NW 13th St, Suite 401 • Gainesville, FL 32609
800-777-2278 • *website:* www.CAPT.org

*Research, training, books, materials, MBTI distribution*

**Consulting Psychologists Press, Inc. (CPP)**
3803 East Bayshore Rd. • Palo Alto, CA 94303
800-624-1765 • *website:* www.CPP-DB.com

*Publisher and distributor of the Myers-Briggs Type Indicator, books, materials, training*

**The Type Reporter, Inc.**
11314 Chapel Rd. • Fairfax Station, VA 22039
703-764-5370

*A psychological type-based publication, published several times a year*

## CHILDREN AND PARENTING

**See Page 61 for videos, slides, and audio cassettes available from Penley and Associates, Inc.**

*Using Type to Explode the Myth of the Ideal Mom*
(Audio Cassette). By Janet P. Penley and Diane W. Stephens. Illustrates important type differences in mothering styles. An audio complement to *The M.O.M.S. Handbook*. 1991. Audio tape. Available through CAPT

*The Developing Child: Using Jungian Type to Understand Children.* By Elizabeth Murphy. Helps adults use type concepts to develop positive, healthy relationships with children and help them succeed. 1993. 155 pages. Paperback. CPP

*KidTypes.* By Susan Scanlon. Real-life examples of the eight personality preferences in children with practical ways parents can apply type knowledge to solve problems. 24 pages. *The Type Reporter, Inc.*

*One of a Kind.* By LaVonne Neff. An easy-to-read book with many practical examples of type within the family — parenting styles, discipline, communication, school success, and marriage. 1988. 187 pages. Paperback. Available through CAPT

*Nurture by Nature: Understand Your Child's Personality Type and Become a Better Parent.* By Paul D. Tieger and Barbara Barron-Tieger. An in-depth look at each of the 16 personality types in preschool, school-aged, and adolescent children, plus tips on what works with children of each type. 1997. 287 pages. Paperback. Little, Brown and Company. Available through CAPT

*Parents' Guide to Type.* By Charles and Constance Meisgeier. Introduces the many uses of type with children and understanding your parenting style. 1989. 32 pages. Booklet. CPP

*People Types and Tiger Stripes: A Practical Guide to Learning Styles.* By Gordon D. Lawrence. Resource for both educators and parents with real-life stories and exercises to explain how type influences learning style. Helps adults understand teacher/student differences and advocate for children in the schools. 1993. 132 pages. Paperback. CAPT

*Relax, Mom, You're Doing a Great Job.* By Susan Scanlon, based on M.O.M.S. Anecdotal profiles of each type mother, plus general reflections on personality type and mothering style. 18 pages. *The Type Reporter, Inc.*

## WORK/CAREERS

***Do What You Are.*** By Paul Tieger and Barbara Barron-Tieger. This guide helps readers of all ages discover the best career for them. Includes specific job search strategies, criteria for satisfaction, and a list of popular occupations for each type. 1992. 330 pages. Paperback. Little Brown and Company. Available through CAPT

***Introduction to Type® in Organizations.*** By Sandra K. Hirsh and Jean M.Kummerow. Applies type concepts to identify the strengths and potential pitfalls of individual work styles, career development, team building, and problem solving. 1987. 32 pages. Booklet. CPP

## GENERAL

***Introduction to Type®.*** By Isabel Briggs Myers. Brief but comprehensive introduction to type theory and the MBTI in everyday language. Profiles, type dynamics, career pathways, problem-solving, verification of scores. 1993. 30 pages. Booklet. CPP

***Type Talk.*** By Otto Kroeger and Janet M. Thuesen. An informative guide for the constructive use of differences in personal relationships, parenting, at work, in teaching and learning. 1988. 289 pages. Paperback. Delacort Press. Available through CAPT

***I'm Not Crazy, I'm Just Not You.*** By Roger R. Pearman and Sarah C. Albritton. A readable, comprehensive introduction to type. Includes how type can be used for personal and social transformation. 1997. 188 pages. Paperback. Davies-Black Publishing. CPP

*Comments or questions for the authors? Thoughts or experiences using this handbook with specific ethnic or racial populations? Fathers? We welcome hearing from you. Call Janet P. Penley at 847-251-4936*
*e-mail: JPMoms@aol.com*
*website: http://www.momsconnection.com*
*Or write Penley and Associates, Inc.*
*604 Maple Ave. Wilmette, IL 60091*

# *Bibliography*

Kroeger, Otto and Janet Thuesen. *Type Talk.* New York: Delacort Press, 1988.

Meisgeier, Charles and Constance. *A Parent's Guide to Type.* Palo Alto, California: Consulting Psychologists Press, Inc., 1989.

Myers, Isabel Briggs. *Introduction to Type®.* Palo Alto, California: Consulting Psychologists Press, Inc., 1987.

Myers, Isabel Briggs and Mary H. McCaulley. *Manual: A Guide to the Development and Use of the Myers-Briggs Type Indicator.* Palo Alto, California: Consulting Psychologists Press, Inc., 1985.

Myers, Isabel Briggs with Peter B. Myers. *Gifts Differing.* Palo Alto, California: Consulting Psychologists Press, Inc., 1993.

Neff, LaVonne. *One of a Kind.* Portland, Oregon: Multnomah Press, 1988.

Page, Earle C. *Looking at Type.* Gainesville, Florida: Center for Applications of Psychological Type, 1983.

Saunders, David R., Isabel Briggs Myers and Katherine C. Briggs. *MBTI Expanded Analysis Report Interpretive Guide.* Palo Alto, California: Consulting Psychologists Press, Inc., 1990.

# *Products for Parents & Professionals*

If you are a parent interested in learning more or a professional committed to supporting and educating parents and families, M.O.M.S. wants to support you. We offer high-quality professional materials for you to use individually or in groups.

### *The M.O.M.S. Handbook: Understanding Your Personality Type in Mothering.*

By Janet P. Penley and Diane W. Stephens. A great hand-out and take-home resource for mothers' groups and workshop participants. Also makes a great gift for baby showers and Mother's Day. Single copy $14. Bulk discounts for groups: four books $48, 10 books $100, 25 books $175.

> Give *The M.O.M.S. Handbook* as a gift!
> Four books $48, 10 for $100, 25 for $175
> Order it for your mothers' group!

### The M.O.M.S. Seminar Video

This 95-minute, two-volume video features women with different mothering styles in intimate at-home settings as they share their stories of using personality type to become better mothers. Plus M.O.M.S. founder Janet Penley leads a M.O.M.S. seminar in a small group. Lively, interactive, personal, natural. Vol.1: introduction to basic M.O.M.S. ideals, overview of Jungian personality type. Vol. 2: mothering styles, with six profiles: ISFJ, ISTJ, ESTP, ENTP, ENTJ, and ENFJ. Use the video in lieu of attending a M.O.M.S. seminar or view it with your friends as a catalyst for discussion. A great training aid for professionals — then use it to make group presentations. Leaders mini-guide included. $125. One week rental $50.

### Parenting Style Presentation Slides and Script

Charming illustrations — as featured throughout this handbook — with brief text for a polished, well-organized presentation. 48 custom four-color slides. Visually engaging and easy to understand. Shows real-life type examples in a light-hearted, affirming way. Fathers as well as mothers included. Each slide accompanied by a detailed script. 48 slides and script $125. 48 color photocopies (11" x 17") and script $150.

### *KidTypes*

Real-life examples of type differences in children. Practical ways parents can use type to solve problems. Four back issues of *The Type Reporter* by Susan Scanlon. $12.

### Audio Cassette Library

Listen to Penley deliver her popular lectures while you drive to work or wait for the carpool. Terrific training aids for professionals — a model for how to present material. Set of 3 for $30, 4 for $40 or $12 each.

*Introduction to M.O.M.S.*
A 90-minute live presentation of M.O.M.S. principles, strengths, struggles for each personality preference. Adds humor, inspiration, more real-life examples, and perspectives on family interactions.

*Reclaiming the Sacred Side of Mothering*
A look at the mothering experience from a spiritual perspective. Includes stories from Penley's own spiritual journey and information from interviews with mothers of different religious backgrounds and personality types.

*How to Put More Fun in Your Mothering*
Mothers who strive to be responsible and do things the right way often struggle with how to enjoy their children. From 100 interviews, Penley offers insights and tips about having more fun as a mother.

*Is It Misbehavior or Personality?*
*New Perspectives on Parent/Child Interactions*
As parents, we often think another family member doesn't care or is making trouble. But that's usually because we don't understand his or her natural way. Descriptions of different type children and stories of parent/child misunderstanding.

### *The M.O.M.S. Connection* Newsletter

Continue your introduction to type with monthly doses of new information about personality type and mothering issues. Gain new perspectives on caring styles, communication, marriage, type development, and parenting. You'll receive six two-page issues over six months. Subscribe for $20.

### Professional Training Workshop

Two days with M.O.M.S. founder and developer Janet Penley. Adds breadth and depth to M.O.M.S. materials. More real-life examples, illustrations and stories. Parenting styles, parent-child interactions, group exercise demonstrations and tips on how to increase your success leading parenting programs. Call for current schedule.

# Order Form

Name _____

Organization_____

Address_____

City_____State_____Zip_____

Phone (daytime)_____E-mail address_____

| Item | Quantity | Price | Total |
|---|---|---|---|
| **The M.O.M.S. Handbook** | | | |
| 1–3 copies | | $14.00 | $ |
| 4–9 copies | | $12.00 | $ |
| 10–24 copies | | $10.00 | $ |
| 25+ copies | | $ 7.00 | $ |
| **The M.O.M.S. Seminar Video** | | $125.00 | $ |
| one week rental | | $ 50.00 (no tax) | $ |
| **Parenting Style Presentation Illustrations and Script** | | | |
| 48 slides and script | | $125.00 | $ |
| 48 color photocopies (11"x17") and script | | $150.00 | $ |
| 48 illustrations on CD-ROM and script | | $145.00 | $ |
| **Audio Cassette Library** | | | |
| *Introduction to M.O.M.S.* | | $12.00 | $ |
| *Reclaiming the Sacred Side of Mothering* | | $12.00 | $ |
| *How to Put More Fun in Your Mothering* | | $12.00 | $ |
| *Is It Misbehavior or Personality?* | | $12.00 | $ |
| (set of three or set of four) | | $30.00 or $40.00 | $ |
| **The M.O.M.S. Connection Newsletter** (6 issues) | | $20.00 (no tax) | $ |
| **Kid Types** | | $12.00 | $ |
| Product subtotal | | | $ |
| Illinois residents add 7.75% sales tax | | | $ |
| Add Shipping and Handling | | | $ |

*$2.50 minimum; $15–25, add 20% of subtotal;*

*$26–125, add 15%; $126–250, add 10%;*

*Over $250, add 5% of subtotal*

**Total Enclosed**                                              $

*prices subject to change without notice*

Visa/MasterCard_____Exp. Date_____

Signature_____

**Make Checks Payable to:** Penley and Associates, Inc.
604 Maple Ave.
Wilmette, IL  60091

*phone:* 847-251-4936 *fax:* 847-251-6998
*e-mail:* JPMoms@aol.com
*website:* http://www.momsconnection.com